LABOUR WELFARE AND SOCIAL SECURITY IN UNORGANISED SECTOR

LABOUR WELFARE AND SOCIAL SECURITY IN UNORGANISED SECTOR

ISBN 978-81-8450-027

Printed in India at NEW ELEGANT PRINTERS
A-47/1, Mayapuri, Phase-I, New Delhi - 110 064

Published by DEEP & DEEP PUBLICATIONS PVT. LTD.
F-159, Rajouri Garden, New Delhi - 110 027 • Phone : 25435369, 25440716
E-mail : [illegible]
Showroom
2/13, Ansari Road, Daryaganj, New Delhi - 110 002 • Tel/Fax : 23245122

LABOUR WELFARE AND SOCIAL SECURITY IN UNORGANISED SECTOR

MEENAKSHI GUPTA
B.Sc., LL.M.
Lecturer in Department of Law,
D.S. College, Aligarh

Foreword by

PROF. (DR.) QAISER HAYAT
Formerly Chairman and Dean, Faculty of Law,
Aligarh Muslim University, Aligarh,
Formerly Director, BG College of Law, Sangrur (Punjab),
Formerly Director, Kawa Global Law School, Raipur (Chattisgarh)

DEEP & DEEP PUBLICATIONS PVT. LTD.
F-159, Rajouri Garden, New Delhi - 110 027

LABOUR WELFARE AND SOCIAL SECURITY IN UNORGANISED SECTOR

ISBN 978-81-8450-027-1

Printed in India at NEW ELEGANT PRINTERS,
A-49/1, Mayapuri, Phase-I, New Delhi - 110 064.

Published by DEEP & DEEP PUBLICATIONS PVT. LTD.,
F-159, Rajouri Garden, New Delhi - 110 027 • Phone : 25435369, 25440916
E-mail : deep98@del3.vsnl.net.in • ddpbooks@yahoo.co.in
Showroom :
2/13, Ansari Road, Daryaganj, New Delhi - 110 002 • Telefax : 23245122

Dedicated

to

Mummy, Papa

and

Sisters

Contents

Foreword

The book is timely. In recent years there has been a marked improvement in the level of awareness about the problems of unorganised sector workers, their poor plight, tough and rough lives. The study assumes great importance as the unorganised sector is a vast and significant segment of Indian economy.

The author has made a comprehensive study of ramparts of defence against tyranny and misrule, exploitation and social injustice. Further she has evaluated social security and welfare measures within the ambit of constitutional and legislative framework and critical judicial approach with a view to have pragmatic strategic benefits.

This in-depth study is significant for all concerns confronted with the problem of unorganised workers. The definition and identification of the problem, elaboration of theories of labour welfare and labour welfare practices in India, critical cases analysis, discussion on why we need social security and obstacles in the implementation of social security measures and suggestions for improvement thereto have made the study specially useful for law students.

PROF. (DR.) QAISER HAYAT

[illegible]

I will always remain indebted to *Prof. Saleem Akhtar* (Ex-Dean and Chairman), *Dr. M. Zaki Neemi*, *Dr. Zahir Ahmad Khan* and *Dr. I.A. Khan* of Aligarh Muslim University for rendering unstinting help, moral support and encouragement.

I acknowledge the kind cooperation of the staff of the Law Seminar and Maulana Azad Library of Aligarh Muslim University for all possible services rendered to me in my present work.

I must record my gratitude to *Prof. Qaiser Hayat*, Formerly Dean and Chairman, Faculty of Law, Aligarh Muslim University, Aligarh, who has given me useful advice, and pleased to give it grace and honour by his "Foreword".

I am greatly indebted to both parents *Shri Hari Mohan Gupta* (M.Sc., D.I.S.) Merchant and Industrialist and *Smt. Madhu Gupta* (B.A.) and also sisters *Dr. Jyotsna Gupta* (M.Sc., Ph.D.), Head of the Department of Plant Pathology, R.B.S. College, Agra, *Miss Poornima Gupta* (LL.M.), Asstt. Public Prosecutor, CBI, New Delhi, *Miss Rimjhim Gupta* (M.A. Eng., PG.D.H.T.) (J.H.T.), Department of Atomic Energy Bhabha Atomic Research Centre, Mumbai and *Miss Neelima Gupta* (M.Tech.) for love, care, inspiration, support and encouragement without which it would have not been possible for me to complete the book.

I sincerely appreciate my friends for their cooperation and help from time to time.

In the end, I also wish to express my appreciation to Deep and Deep Publication Pvt. Ltd., New Delhi for their courtesy and constant help and cooperation in expediting the publication of book.

MEENAKSHI GUPTA

Preface

The problems of unorganised sector are among the basic elements in the economic and social life of any country and have commanded growing attention not only to the industrialist and work people, but of the Government and the public. The main purpose of this book is to highlight the magnitude of the problems of the unorganised sector and to provide labour welfare and social security in unorganised sector. Therefore, a proper understanding of the problems such as Unorganised Sector: Problem of Definition and Identification, Categories of Unorganised Sector, Labour Welfare Activities, Agencies for Labour Welfare Work, Social Security and its Scope, Social Security: Unorganised Sector, Legislation Relating to Unorganised Sector, Judicial Response which has been discussed in the present book is very much required. It is hoped that this book would be of valuable help to the individual and groups who intend to work towards improving the quality of life of these teeming millions.

I feel indebted to all those authors whose publication on the subject of unorganised sector has benefitted me in the preparation of this book. A bibliography at the end of the book indicates the works studied and authors whose views are incorporated and analysed in it. The book is extensively based on various Reports and Standard Journals.

I am highly honoured to *Dr. Zaheeruddin*, Reader, Faculty of Law, Aligarh Muslim University, Aligarh for constant supervision, unceasing interest, critical suggestions and never ending encouragement.

I will always remain indebted to *Prof. Saleem Akhtar* (Ex-Dean and Chairman), *Dr. M.Z.M. Nomani, Dr. Zubair Ahmad Khan* and *Dr. I.A. Khan* of Aligarh Muslim University for rendering unstinting help, moral support and encouragement.

I acknowledge the kind cooperation of the staff of the Law Seminar and Maulana Azad Library of Aligarh Muslim University for all possible services rendered to me in my present work.

I must record my gratitude to *Prof. Qaiser Hayat*, Formerly Dean and Chairman, Faculty of Law, Aligarh Muslim University, Aligarh, who has given me useful advices and pleased to give it grace and honour by his "Foreword".

I am greatly indebted to both parents *Shri Hari Mohan Gupta* (M.Sc., D.I.S.), Merchant and Industrialist and *Smt. Madhu Gupta* (B.A.) and also sisters *Dr. Jhilmil Gupta* (M.Sc., Ph.D.), Head of the Department of Plant Pathology, R.B.S. College, Agra, *Miss Poornima Gupta* (LL.M.), Asstt. Public Prosecutor, CBI, New Delhi, *Miss Rimjhim Gupta* (M.A. Eng., P.G.D.H.T.) (J.H.T.), Department of Atomic Energy, Bhabha Atomic Research Centre, Mumbai and *Miss Neelima Gupta* (M.Tech.) for love, care, inspiration, support and encouragement without which it would have not been possible for me to complete the book.

I sincerely appreciate my friends for their cooperation and help from time to time.

In the end, I also wish to express my appreciation to Deep and Deep Publication Pvt. Ltd., New Delhi for their courtesy and constant help and co-operation in expediting the publication of book.

Meenakshi Gupta

MEENAKSHI GUPTA

Abbreviations

A.I.R.	All India Reporter
AITUC	All India Trade Union Congress
A.P.	Andhra Pradesh
BMS	Bhartiya Mazdoor Sangh
CTTU	Centre of Indian Trade Unions
CLRA	Contract Labour Regulation and Abolition
CORP.	Corporation
GOVT.	Government
GUJ.	Gujarat
H.C.	High Court
HMS	Hind Mazdoor Sabha
ILC	Indian Labour Conference
ILO	International Labour Organisation
IRC	Industrial Relations Commission
INTUC	Indian National Trade Union Congress
ISMW	Inter State Migrant Workmen
LLJ	Labour Law Journal
LTD.	Limited
M.P.	Madhya Pradesh
MNC	Multi National Company

NCL	National Commission on Labour
NGO	Non Governmental Organisation
ORIS	Orissa
SAIL	Steel Authority of India
S.C.	Supreme Court
SCC	Supreme Court Cases
S.C.J.	Supreme Court Journal
SCR	Supreme Court Report
SNCL	Second National Commission on Labour
U.P.	Uttar Pradesh
UN	United Nations
U.N.O.	United Nations Organisations
UTUC	United Trade Union Congress
UTUC (LS)	United Trade Union Congress-Lenin Sarani

Introduction

Unorganised sector is a vast and significant segment of Indian economy in terms of its economic worth through their economic contribution and the growing number of the workers the sector engages. The unorganised sector in our country employs around 37 crore workers and is fast expanding as a result of the liberalisation policies. A vast majority of them—23.7 crore—are engaged in agriculture. Out of the rest, 4.1 crore work in manufacturing, 3.7 crore each in services and trade, and around 1.7 crore work in construction. The unorganised sector workers are literally everywhere, in fields, in homes, on streets, in small workshops, in forest-everywhere. Over 90% of labour force work in this sector.

Unorganised sector could be described as that part of the workforce 'who have not been able to organise in pursuit of a common objective because of constraints such as (a) casual nature of employment, (b) ignorance and illiteracy, (c) small size of establishments with low capital investment per person employed, (d) scattered nature of establishments and (e) superior strength of the employer operating singly or in combination.'

The unorganised sector comprises the various categories such as (a) those who are employed on a more or less regular basis, in establishments which are outside the scope of the existing social security legislation, (b) those who are employed as casual labour, intermittently on contracts, with uncertain employment and income, (c) those who are own account workers and producers, including small and marginal farmers, who may occasionally hire the labour of others, (d) those who do a variety of jobs from day to day, from season to season, and often even within the same day, (e) those who are seeking work as migrant labour, (f) those who worked but can no longer work.

Unlike the organised sector, in unorganised sector workers have not acquired a high profile, tasted the benefits that can be gained from organisation, or derived the advantageous flowing from high visibility. The employments in which they are engaged vary from the most unskilled jobs like stone breaking or collecting minor forest produce, to sophisticated jobs in software technology or infosystems. The vast majority of the workers are extremely poor. It can also be said that 90 percent or more of the poor in our country are in the unorganised sector: employed, underemployed or unemployed. They are not only poor and marginally employed, but are deprived and discriminated against. Many of them belong to the Schedule Castes and Tribes for whom our Constitution has prescribed special consideration and protection. Their incomes are so low and that they cannot provide for, or buy social security, they cannot even buy food or clothing. Many of them are victims of the system of 'bonded slavery' and are described as bonded labour. Many of them are contract workers, home-based workers, semi-skilled and unskilled, home-based skilled artisans, and a section of the self-employed involved in job such as vending, rag picking, rickshaw pulling. Then come the agricultural workers, rural non-agricultural labour, khadi and village industries workers, construction workers, migrant labour and those in manual and helper jobs. The categories naturally will be illustrative rather than exhaustive.

The 'unorganised sector' has been criticised as a low productivity area where the earnings are meagre. But in absolute terms, this sector contributes more to the economy and employment in India. Nine tenth of the India's population is surviving on employments in the unorganised sector. Thus, inspite of their considerable contribution, the unorganised sector lack adequate protection. They are exploited in many ways. They are exposed to all the vagaries of climate and weather such as scorching sun, heavy rain, and chilly winter while at work. Workers are exposed to serious health hazards which affect their longevity. Workers in this sector do not get social and other benefits as their counterparts in the organised sector do. In other words, it can be said that effective protection and welfare for the unorganised sector is a shade more difficult and complicated.

The issue, before a developing countries like India is to provide adequate welfare measures and social protection for the vast majority of the population engaged in unorganised sector activities.

Welfare is the broad concept. It connotes a condition of well-being, happiness, satisfaction, conservation and development of human resources. The term welfare applied to labour, therefore, refers to adoption of measures which aim at promoting the physical, psychological and general well-being of the working population. The basic aim of welfare services in an industry is to improve the living and working conditions of workers and their families because the worker's well-being cannot be achieved in isolation of his family.[1] The concept of welfare is necessarily dynamic, bearing a different interpretation from country to country and from time to time and even in the same country, according to its value system, social institution, degree of industrialisation and general level of social and economic development. According to ILO classification welfare amenities are (i) latrines and urinals, (ii) washing and bathing facilities, (iii) creches, (iv) rest shelters and canteens, (v) arrangements for drinking water, (vi) arrangements for prevention of Fatigue, (vii) health services including occupational safety, (vii) administrative arrangement within a plant or establishment to look after welfare, (ix) uniforms and protective cooling and (x) shift allowance.[2]

The usefulness of welfare work in India cannot be over-emphasised. Welfare measures will improve the physique, intelligence, morality and standard of living of the workers which in turn, will improve their efficiency and productivity. A high standard of efficiency can be expected only from persons who are properly trained, properly housed, properly fed and properly clothed.

In India, there are several agencies through which various labour welfare measures are undertaken in the interest of labour. Welfare measures are undertaken by Central and State Governments. Labour legislation has been enacted by Central and State Governments which has laid down the minimum standard of employment and working class. The labour policy set out in the Five Year Plans since independence was based on the belief that the basic needs of workers for food, clothing and shelter must be satisfied. Besides, Central and State Governments, employers, workers trade unions, and social organisation also work as agencies for providing facilities to the workers.

Social security is a basic need of all people regardless of employment in which they work and live. It is an important form of social protection. It should be begun with birth and should continue till death. In modern era, social security is the *sine qua non* of the economic system and important tool to strike at the roots of poverty, unemployment and disease. Basically, the idea is to guarantee security of income whenever normal income ceases and in addition to provide medical care and financial help in bringing up large families. Wherever such schemes are financed from general revenues, they are called *"social assistance schemes."* Where they are financed on contributory basis they are called *"social insurance schemes." However, the term social security includes both social assistance and social insurance schemes.*

The main risk or insecurity to which human life is responsible and in relation to which an organised society can afford relief to the helpless individuals are the incidents occurring right from childhood up to old age and death, which include mainly sickness, invalidity due to maternity, accident and occupational diseases, unemployment old age etc. In addition to labour welfare and economic protection of workers, social security covers also socio-economic progress and development of the weaker classes. Thus, social security has assumed considerable importance in the recent years.

Several schemes have been evolved in India through legislations and policies to provide social security to the workers in the unorganised sector. Some of the important schemes are *Integrated Rural Development Programme, Rural Group Life Insurance Scheme, Old Age Pension Scheme, National Agricultural Insurance Scheme, Krishi Shramik Samajik Suraksha*

Yojana, Shiksha Sahayog Yojana, Orissa Unemployment Assistance Scheme, The Jawahar Gram Samriddi Yojana, Swarnjayanti Gram Swarozgar Yojana, Employment Assurance Scheme, Pradhan Mantri Gramodaya Yojana, Samagra Awaas Yojana.

Recently, in February 22, 2004, the Prime Minister Atal Bihari Vajpayee launched a social security scheme for unorganised sector offering health insurance and old age pension to them and underlined the need to bring labourers under the organised sector.

Beside this in November 14, 2004 National Food For Work Programme has been launched to provide additional supplementary wage employment in the identified 150 most backward districts of the country.

In year 2005, Rajiv Gandhi Shramik Kalayan Yojana, National Rural Health Mission, Bhoomi Sena Scheme, Tamil Nadu Chief Minister's Farmers Security Scheme has been launched.

Constitution of India offers protection and social security to all citizens of India. It is obvious that the workers in the unorganised sector are as much entitled to protection and welfare or social security as citizens in any other groups. The Indian Constitution with its "paediatric" conscience makes special provisions under Articles 14, 15, 19, 21, 23, 24, 41, 42, 43 and 47 to the unorganised sector.

There are legislations that apply wholly or partly to unorganised sector. These legislations are: *The Factories Act, 1948, the Minimum Wages Act, 1948, the Payment of Wages Act, 1936, the Workmen Compensation Act, 1923,* which are applicable to the workers in the unorganised sector where there is an identifiable employer-employee relationship. In some of the employments or avocations, contractors are engaged, and this results in a situation in which the principal employer does not come into the picture such as in building/construction activity, beedi rolling, mining (particularly stone mining) or quarrying and various other occupations. There workers are sometimes covered under more than one law e.g. the *Contract Labour (Regulation and Abolition) Act, 1970* as well as under one specific law or another like *Beedi and Cigar Workers (Conditions of Employment) Act, 1966, Building and Other Construction Workers' (Regulation of Employment and Conditions of Service) Act, 1996, the Mines Act, 1952. Plantation Labour Act, 1951* regulates, for the first time, the condition of work of plantation workers and provides for their welfare. *Dock Workers' (Regulation of Employment) Act, 1948* enacted for the purpose of the welfare of the dock workers. The vast majority of the migrant workers fall in the unorganised sector. Hence, the Inter-State Migrant Workmen (Regulation of Employment and Conditions of Service) Act, 1979 was enacted to regulate the employment and conditions of service of interstate migrant workers.

There is a wide variety of employments in the unorganised sector. It is difficult to have separate laws for each employment. Hence the Second National Commission on Labour suggested a umbrella legislation that covers whatever is basic and common and leaves room for supplementary legislation or rules where specific area demand special attention.

The Unorganised Sector Workers (Employment and Welfare) Bill, 2003 is the reaction of the Indian ruling classes, to the present crisis. The Bill is the logical outcome of the Second National Labour Commission's recommendations. The aims of the Bill are to obtain recognition of all workers in the unorganised sector, to ensure a minimum level of economic security, to ensure a minimum level of social security, to expedite removal of the poverty of these workers through their work, protecting their means of employment and income. It may be observed that the Bill, 2003 need to be modified to give more protection to unorganized worker.The Unorganised Workers' Bill, 2004 being redrafted to promote well beings to workers in unorganized sector. The Unorganised Sector Workers Bill, 2004 is broad that covers workers scattered throughout the length and breadth of this country. The Bill focuses more on workers who work for an employer.

The National Comission for enterprises in the unorganized sector has recently drafted the two new Bills—The Unorganised Sector Workers Social Security Bill, 2005 and The Unorganised Sector Workers (Conditions of Work and Livelihood Promotion) Bill, 2005. These Bill have been formulated after examing the Unorganised Sector Workers' Bill, 2004, prepared by the Ministry of Labour and Employment, Government of India and the Draft of Unorganised Sector Workers' Social Security Bill prepared by the National Advisory Council. The aims of the two bills was to ensure the smooth and effective implementation of social security schemes for the unorganized sector workers.

The Unorganised Sector Workers' Social Security Bill, 2005 would cover approximately 30 crores workers in the unorganized sector with a monthly income up to Rs. 5,000. The Unorganised Sector Workers (Conditions of Work and Livelihood Promotion) Bill, 2005 deals with condition of work, livelihood promotion, addresses the issues relating to provide a basic minimum standard on hours of work, payment of minimum wages, bonded labour and child labour.

Recently, The Parliament has passed the historical National Rural Employment Guarantee Act, 2005, that guarantees 100 days of wage employment in a year to every rural household whose adult members are willing to do unskilled manual work. Intially, the Act will be in operation in 200 districts and will be extended to the whole country by 2010.

The Judiciary in India under it policy for attainment of social justice has been very attendant to give effect the rights of unorganised labour. The role of Supreme Court in protecting poor and the weakest of the weak, unorganised labour is very appreciating. Several rights of workers in unorganised sector have been recognised by Supreme Court of India in its various judicial decisions. *The Crown Aluminium Works,*[3] *Peoples Union for Democratic Rights,*[4] *Sanjit Roy,*[5] *Salal Hydroelectric Project,*[6] *Bandhu Mukti Morcha,*[7] *Neerja Chaudhary*[8] *and two cases of M.C. Mehta*[9] *etc.* touched the issue of labour welfare, freedom from bondage and dignity, social security, health and children of the country.

In various cases, the Court have dealt with the issue, namely whether the workers employed by the contractor in canteen may be treated as employees of the principal employer?

After the commencement of the *Contract Labour (Regulation and Abolition) Act, 1970, Air India case*[10] *of 1997* is the landmark judgement given by the Apex Court. In this case it was held that though there is no provision in the CLRA Act, 1970 for absorption of the employees whose contract labour system stood abolished under the Act. But the Act does not prohibit the corporation to absorb them in regular service and that is the mandate of the Constitution in Article 21.

On September 30, 2001 a Constitutional bench of the Supreme Court in *Steel Authority of India case*[11] delivered a momentous judgement having a bearing on contract labour system. The Court has re-opened several important issues earlier decided by a three judge bench in *Air India case* and overruled the same prospectively, thereby, *inter alia*, denied the right of contract labour to be absorbed, on abolition of contract labour system, a right earlier created by another three judge bench by judicial legislation. The principles evolved in the judgement are pregnant with tremendous liability and would bring anomalous results.

The laws, schemes and welfare systems that are proposed for unorganised sector workers cannot be effective unless they themselves are conscious of the laws, and acquire the strength to ensure that laws are brought into force; unless there are effective means to implement; unless judiciary played its significant role; unless breaches of the law are punished with deterrent penalties, and unless the organs of public opinion and movements and organisations mount vigil, and intercede to ensure that the provisions of the laws and welfare system are acted upon.

The present study makes a humble attempt to understand what unorganised sector means and to study categories of unorganised sector. An effort has been made how to provide social security and welfare measures for the unorganised sector. An attempt is made here to evaluate the schemes that are in operation in India with a view to suggest certain strategies to enhance the social protection for this sector. The study is a modest presentation of constitutional and legislative framework culminating towards pregmatic strategies. In this study an effort has been made to discuss the attitude of judiciary towards the rights of the workers engage in unorganised sector.

Chapter I deals with *Unorganised Sector: Problem of Definition and Identification*. It tells about the difficulty which arises in the definition and identification of unorganised sector.

Chapter II deals with *Categories of Unorganised Sector*. This chapter refer to categories of workers engaged in the unorganised sector and the problems confronted by them.

Chapter III deals with *Labour Welfare Activities*. It tells us why we need to labour welfare work in India and what is the concept and scope of labour welfare. It also throws light on theories of labour welfare, principles of labour welfare and labour welfare practices in India.

Chapter IV deals with *Agencies for Labour Welfare Work*. It tells us what welfare measures are undertaken by Central and

State Governments, Municipalities, Employers, Voluntary Organisations, Workers' Organisations in the interest of labour.

Chapter V deals with *Social Security and its Scope*. It throws light on evolution, meaning, constituents, and scope of social security.

Chapter VI deals with *Social Security: Unorganised Sector*. It tells why we need to social security for unorganised sector and what is obstacles in the extension of social security. It also discuss constitutional provisions which provided protection to unorganised sector. It briefly highlight the major promotional schemes which are in operation in India to provide social protection to unorganised sector and suggest certain strategies needed to enhance the social protection for the unorganised sector.

Chapter VII deals with *Legislations Relating to Unorganised Sector*. In this chapter an attempt is made to see whether existing legislations cover the entire area of unorganised sector, whether they are adequate to give even the minimum of protection, safety and social security to vast and varied workforce in the unorganised sector and whether the problem of variety can be solved or addressed by enacting an umbrella law.

Chapter VIII deals with *Judicial Response*. A critical analysis of various cases has been made in this chapter.

Chapter IX deals with *Conclusion and Suggestions*. A summarization of the present study is attempted and a few suggestions are proposed therein.

Notes and References

1. Report of the Committee on Labour Welfare, (1969) p. 5.
2. Report of the First National Commission on Labour (1969) pp. 111-12.
3. Crown Aluminium Works *v.* Their Workmen, (1958), 1.L.L.J.1.
4. Peoples Union for Democratic Rights *v.* Union of India, (1982), 2 L.L.J. 454.
5. Sanjit Roy *v.* State of Rajasthan, AIR 1983 S.C. 1155.
6. Salal Hydro Electric Project *v.* State of J and K, (1983) 2 SCC 181.
7. Bandhu Mukti Morcha *v.* Union of India, A.I.R. 1984 S.C. 802.
8. Neerja Chaudhary *v.* State of M.P., A.I.R. 1984 SC 1099.
9. M.C. Mehta *v.* State of Tamil Nadu, AIR 1991 SC 417.
10. Air India Statutory Corp. *v.* United Labour Union, 1997 LLR 288.
11. Steel Authority of India. *v.* National Union Water Front Workers and Others, 2001 LLR 961.

1

Unorganised Sector : Problem of Definition and Identification

The unorganised sector workers are literally everywhere, in fields, in homes, on streets, in small workshops, in forests-everywhere. Over 90% of our labour force work in this sector. Unlike the organised sector, in unorganised sector workers have not acquired a high profile, tasted the benefits that can be gained from organisation, or derived the advantageous flowing from high visibility. In the unorganised sector, the workers are engaged in a variety of occupations or employments, ranging from those like forest workers, tribals trying to follow traditional vocations within their traditional habitats, and fishermen who venture out to sea in vulnerable canoes, to those who are working in their homes with software, or assembling parts for a highly sophisticated product. Many of them are victims of invisibility.

The 'unorganised sector' has been criticised as a low productivity area where the earnings are meagre. But in absolute terms, this sector contributes more to the economy and employment in India. Thus, inspite of their considerable contribution, the unorganised sector lack adequate protection through labour legislation. Workers in this sector do not get social security and other benefits as their counterparts in the organised sector do. In other words it can be said that effective protection and welfare for the unorganised sector is a shade more difficult and complicated, it is only because of the problem of definition and identification of unorganised sector.

The first difficulty is that unorganised sector could not be defined or described on the basis of the nature of the work that workers or employees in the sector are engaged in, because, the sector has tribal forest workers as well as home-based, info-tech and software workers. It cannot be based on the number of employees in undertakings because it covers agricultural workers, craftsmen, home-based workers, self-employed workers, workers in weavers' cooperatives, as well as workers in small scale industries where the workforce can be counted on one's fingers. It cannot be based on the level of organisation because some of the enterprises may have very few workers, and even these may be working in a dispersed manner with hardly any organisational link or interaction with each other, sometimes because of the nature of the work, and sometimes because of the geographical or locational dispersal of the workers pursuing the same vocation. How then can we define the sector? It would seem that the vocations, employments and conditions of work are so varied and disparate that it is impossible to provide protection and welfare to all workers in all these sub-sectors, with one uniform law or one uniform system for welfare and social security.[1]

It has often been pointed out, and perhaps universally accepted, that there are areas in the unorganised sector where it is difficult to identify an 'employer', and hence, an employer-employee relationship, which the law can attempt to channelise or influence by defining rights and responsibilities, and building-up a system of social security on a contributory basis. The employer of the construction worker or the brick kiln worker can perhaps be identified as a direct employer or a contractor. An employer can perhaps be identified even in the case of a worker who collects minor forest produce, as one, who works for a contractor or the forest department. But no employer can be identified for a fisherman who casts his net into a pond or stream, or for a woman who spin of weaves, or tends livestock at home, to sell sruplus milk to a co-operative or to a consumer who is her neighbour. This difficulty in identifying an employer-employee relationship has its corollaries.[2]

The concept of an unorganised sector began to receive world-wide attention in the early 1970s, when the *International Labour Organisation* initiated serious efforts to identify and study the area through its World Employment Programme Missions in Africa. Since then, the informal sector has been the subject of several studies and seminars covering various aspects like its size, employment potential, its relationship with the formal sector, technological levels etc. In 1987, the Director General of the ILO submitted a report to the International Labour Conference on the "Dilemma of the Informal Sector." In it he referred to the role of this sector in promoting employment, the absence of adequate laws for providing protection to workers in this sector, and the scope for application of international labour standard in this area.[3]

In India, however, the term unorganised sector is of recent origin, and has been in use only during the last two decades. A number of studies have been conducted to assess the size and employment structure of the sector in different urban localities by agencies like the Institute of Applied Manpower Research etc. during the late eighties and early nineties.[4]

The *First National Commission on Labour*, under the chairmanship of justice Gajendragadkar, defined the unorganised sector as that part of as the workforce 'who have not been able to organise in pursuit of a common objective because of constraints such as (a) casual nature of employment, (b) ignorance and illiteracy, (c) small size of establishments with low capital investment per person employed, (d) scattered nature of establishments and (e) superior strength of the employer operating singly or in combination.' The Commission listed 'illustrative' categories of unorganised labour: 'These are: (i) contract labour including construction workers; (ii) casual labour; (iii) labour employed in small scale industry; (iv) handloom/power-loom workers; (v) beedi and cigar workers; (vi) employees in shops and commercial establishments; (vii) sweepers and scavenger; (viii) workers in tanneries; (ix) tribal labour; and (x) 'other unprotected labour.'[5]

The *National Commission on Self-Employed Women*, setup in 1987 under the chairpersonship of Smt. Ela R. Bhatt, included in their terms of reference, the women workers in the unorganised sector. This report characterised the unorganised sector as one in which women 'do arduous work as wage earners, piece-rate workers, casual labour and paid and unpaid family labour. The economic and social conditions of these women are dismissal.' The report also observed that 'the unorganised sector is characterized by a high incidence of casual labour mostly doing intermittent jobs at extremely low wages or doing their own account work at very uneconomical returns. There is a total lack of job security and social security benefits. The areas of exploitation are high, resulting in long hours, unsatisfactory work conditions, and occupational health hazards.'[6]

The *National Council for Applied Economic Research (NCAER)* and *Self-Employed Women's Association (SEWA)* conducted a joint workshop on the subject of defining the informal sector in March-April 1997. The Central Statistical Organisation formed an expert Group on the informal sector (Delhi Group) to suggest a definition of the informal sector. In the NCAER-SEWA workshop, a Gujarat-based Group of experts on Estimation of the Informal Sector proposed a definition for the informal sector based on employment. According to the Group, the informal sector included all workers in informal enterprises, some workers in formal enterprises, self-employed workers, and those doing contract work for informal or formal sector enterprises and contractors.[7] The NCAER-SEWA workshop raised doubts on the enterprise-based definition of the informal sector. It pointed out that such a definition would leave out workers who were working on contract basis. It said that the definition should be based on activities and ranks of the self-employed producing non-tradeable services and items for the local markets. It further said that the National Accounting must cover the informal sector which included home-based workers, artisans groups and contract workers, besides workers in the unorganised sector of services manufacturing and agriculture.

Definition and Identifiable Characteristics

It may be seen from the above observations that the unorganised sector is too vast to remain within the confines of a conceptual definition. Hence, descriptive means are often used to identify the unorganised or informal sector.[8]

In India, the term 'unorganised sector' is used commonly in all official records and analyses. It is defined as the residual of the organised sector. The term 'organised' is generally used to enterprises or employees in which 10 or more employees work together. Problems of underestimation and insufficient coverage in the unorganised sector lead to further problems in deriving the residual estimate of the unorganised sector. Therefore, definitions based on the residual approach, that consider the organised sector as employing 10 or more workers and the unorganised sector as the residual, no longer seem to be dependable. Many new types of enterprises and employments that have emerged in recent years, have to be taken into account.[9]

The unorganised sector is very diverse. Many efforts have been made to identify the characteristics of employments or undertakings in the sector. But none of the characteristics can be termed as crucial in defining the sector. However, some of the important characteristics of employments or undertakings in the sector are:

(a) low scale of organisation;
(b) operation of labour relations on a casual basis, or on the basis of kinship or personal relations;
(c) small own account (household) or family—owned enterprises or micro enterprises;
(d) ownership of fixed and other assets by self;
(e) risking of finance capital by self;
(f) involvement of family labourers;
(g) production expenditure indistinguishable from household expenditures and use of capital goods;
(h) easy entry and exist;
(i) free mobility within the sector;
(j) use of indigenous resources and technology;
(k) unregulated or unprotected nature;
(l) absence of fixed working hours;
(m) lack of security of employment and other social security benefits;
(n) use of labour intensive technology;

(o) lake of support from Government;
(p) workers living in slums and squatter areas;
(q) lack of housing and access to urban services; and
(r) high percentage of migrant labour.[10]

The unorganised sector is in no way an independent and exclusive sector. It is linked to, or in many cases, dependent on the organised sector and the rest of the economy through a variety of linkages. It depends on the organised sector for raw materials and other capital requirements, generation of employment, marketing facilities, and so on. The subcontracting model is used by the formal sector for engaging labour in the unorganised sector.[11]

It cannot be denied that the unorganised sector does not get enough protection through labour legislation. Despite the existence of labour laws, for various reasons, the workers in this sector do not get social security and other benefits, as do their counterparts in the formal sector. Here, workers are highly exploited by entrepreneurs They are employed on a casual basis. With the exception of very few cases, there is hardly any trade union or other institutional machinery to fight for the workers. Up to now, collective bargaining has not been able to get any visible space in the unorganised sector. As the workers in the unorganised sector, particularly women, have not been able to organise themselves, they are further discriminated against in the sector. Thus, this is a sector in which workers do not have protection or adequate bargaining power.[12]

In the organised sector too, there is a section of permanent workers who are getting casualised and contractualised as a consequence of the new economic and industrial policies. At the same time, there are sections of workers in the unorganised sector, who are organised and unionised as, for example, the head load workers in some of the industrial and trade centres. Thus, workers in the unorganised sector include all the workers of the unorganised sector as well as the casual and contract workers in the organised sector who, for one reason or another, have failed to get the benefits of protective legislation or laws or social security.[13]

In a sense, all workers, who are not covered by the existing Social Security Laws like *Employees State Insurance Act, 1948,*

Employee Provident Fund and Miscellaneous Provisions Act, 1952, Payment of Gratuity Act, 1972 and Maternity Benefit Act, 1961, can be considered as part of the unorganised sector.[14]

Perhaps, then, the unorganised sector is a term that eludes definition. Its main features can be identified, and sectors and processes where unorganised labour is used can be listed, though not exhaustively. Apprentices, casual and contract workers, home-based artisans, and a section of self-employed persons involved in jobs such as vending, rag picking and rickshaw pulling come in the unorganised sector. Agricultural workers, construction workers, migrant labour and those who perform manual and helper jobs also come in the category of unorganised sector workers. Workers who depend directly or indirectly on natural resources that are open or common property-based are also included in the unorganised sector provided:

(a) that it does not include any such person who is subject to the three armed forces Acts or prison services;
(b) and that they are not employed as permanent workers in :

- factories, as defined in Section 2 (m) of the Factories Act of 1948,
- plantations, as defined in Section 2(f) of the Plantations Labour Act, 1951,
- mines, as defined in Section 2(j) of the Mines Act of 1952, and
- Shops and commercial establishments, as defined by the different State Acts.[15]

Other casual and contract workers in defence establishments, factories, plantations, mines and shops and commercial establishments, who for some reason do not enjoy the benefits of the Social Security Laws, should however, be regarded as part of the unorganised sector workforce. The form of employment or the labour relationship is important in demarcating different sectors. However, conventional labour laws do not define most of them as employees or workers, because a principal employer is unidentifiable in most of these sectors.[16]

In India, the official definition of the informal sector enterprises consists of Directory Establishments that employ at least six persons but not more than nine, Non-Directory Establishments which employ five persons or less, and Own Account Enterprises that employ oneself. Officially, these constitute the unorganised sector of industries. However, the available database and hence, the modes of estimation of the unorganised sector workforce are not so dependable.[17]

The sample study of economic activities has brought out some general characteristics of enterprises or employment in the unorganised sector. It has been seen:

(a) It is in general a low wage and low wage and low earning sector.
(b) Women constitute an important section of the workers in this sector.
(c) Family labour is engaged in some occupations such as home-based ones.
(d) Economic activities, which engage child labour, fall within this sector.
(e) Migrant labour is involved in some sub-sectors.
(f) Piece-rate payment, home-based work and contractual work are increasing trends in this sector.
(g) Direct recruitment is on the decline. Some employees are engaged through contractors. An increasing trend to recruit workers through contractor is visible in areas of home-based work. There is a sort of convergence of home-based work and engagement in work through contractors.
(h) If some kinds of employment are seasonal, some others are intermittent. As such, underemployment is a serious problem.
(i) Most jobs are, for the greater part, on a casual basis.
(j) Both employed and self-employed workers can be found in a number of occupations.
(k) Workers are not often organised into trade unions. The self-employed are seldom organised into associations. There is not much recourse to collective bargaining.

(l) There are many co-operatives of self-employed workers.

(m) Very often, others supply raw materials, production by self-employed workers, therefore, becomes dependent on, or linked with enterprises or individuals active in other sectors.

(n) Debt bondage is very common among the employed as well as the self-employed workers in the unorganised sector.

(o) The self-employed have less access to capital. Whatever capital they manage, is mostly from non-banking and usurious sources, especially from the trader–contractor.

(p) Health hazards exist in a majority of occupations.[18]

From the above observation it is clear that unorganised sector could not be defined and identified solely on the basis of the nature of work of the workers or on the basis of the number of employees in the undertaking and also not on the level of organisation. The unorganised sector is too vast to remain within the confines of a conceptual definition. Hence many efforts have been made to identify the characteristics of employments or undertakings in the sector. But none of the characteristics can be termed as crucial in defining the sector. However, it can be said these are main features such as low wages and low earnings, high percentage of employment of women, employment of family labour, child labour, migrant labour, piece rate payments, home based work or contractual work, seasonal or intermittent employment, lack of organisation into trade unions, casual and multiple jobs, existence of debt bondage, existence of cooperatives of self-employed workers, dependence on others for supply of raw material, less access to capital, existence of health hazards are often used to define and identify the unorganised sector.

Notes and References

1. Report of the Second National Commission on Labour, 2002, 7.5.
2. *Ibid.*, 2002, 7.6.
3. *Ibid.*, 2002, 7.9.
4. *Ibid.*, 2002, 7.10.

5. Report of the First National Commission on Labour, 1969, p. 417.
6. Report of the Second National Commission on Labour, 2002, p. 7.12.
7. Kantor, 1997, Cited by Report of the Second National Commission on Labour, 2002, pp. 598-599.
8. Report of the Second National Commission on Labour, 2002, 7.15.
9. *Ibid.*, 2002, 7.17.
10. *Ibid.*, 2002, 7.18.
11. *Ibid.*, 2002, 7.22.
12. *Ibid.*, 2002, 7.23.
13. *Ibid.*, 2002, 7.24.
14. *Ibid.*, 2002, 7.25.
15. *Ibid.*, 2002, 7.26.
16. *Ibid.*, 2002, 7.27.
17. *Ibid.*, 2002, 7.28.
18. *Ibid.*, 2002, 7.30.

2

Categories of Unorganised Sector

Unorganised sector could be described as that part of the workforce 'who have not been able to organise in pursuit of a common objective because of constraints such as (a) casual nature of employment, (b) ignorance and illiteracy, (c) small size of establishments with low capital investment per person employed, (d) scattered nature of establishments and (e) superior strength of the employer operating singly or in combination.'

Unorganised sector is vast and varied. This sector including the agricultural sector account for more than 92% of the total workforce in the country, i.e. around one third of India's population. Nine tenth of the India's population is surviving on employments in the Unorganised sector. The employments in which they are engaged vary from the most unskilled jobs like stone breaking or collecting minor forest produce, to sophisticated jobs in software technology or infosystems. The vast majority of the workers are extremely poor. It can also be said that 90 percent or more of the poor in our country are in the Unorganised sector: employed, underemployed or unemployed. They are not only poor and marginally employed, but are deprived and discriminated against. Many of them belong to the Schedule Castes and Tribes for whom our Constitution has prescribed special consideration and protection. Their incomes are so low that they cannot provide for, or buy social security; they cannot even buy food or clothing. Many of them are victims of the system of 'bonded slavery' and are described as bonded labour. Many of them are contract workers, home-based workers, semi-skilled and unskilled, home-based skilled artisans, and a section of the self-employed involved in job such as vending, rag picking, rickshaw pulling. Then come the agricultural workers, rural non-agricultural labour, khadi and village industries workers, construction workers, migrant labour and those in manual and helper jobs. The categories naturally will be illustrative rather than exhaustive.

1. MINES AND QUARRY WORKERS

According to the *Mines Act, 1952* any person who works in a mine as Manager or who works under appointment by an owner's agent or manager of a mine with or without knowledge of such person whether for wages or not is treated as 'employed in a mine.' The Act, therefore, covers persons employed in mining operations including in transporting minerals to the point of dispatch, or within the mining area, or in any operations relating to the development of the mine or in any operation of servicing, maintenance, or repair of any machinery used in the mine, or in any office in the mine or in any welfare health or conservancy service required to be provided under the Mines Act, or any watch and ward staff within the premises of the mine (excluding the residential area), or in any kind of work whatsoever which is preparatory or incidental to or connected with mining operations. But persons employed in any construction activity, which is not connected with the mine, are not treated as persons employed in a mine.

The term 'mine' is also very widely defined in the Act. It not only covers all borings, bore holes, oil wells, shafts and inclines, and open cast working but also all adits, level planes, machinery, railways and tramways belonging to the mine; all workshops and stores situated within the mines; all transformers and sub-stations in a mine meant for supplying electricity solely for the purpose of mine; all premises used for depositing sand or other material for use in a mine, etc.[1]

Mines can be divided broadly into three categories:

(a) Public sector mines whether worked independently or as captive mines of public sector enterprises such as Coal India Ltd., Steel Authority of India Ltd., The oil fields of the Oil and Natural Gas Commission, Oil India Ltd etc. The private sector captive mines of some of the larger steel and other smelting plants such as ferro manganese, ferro chrome, cement, etc. can also be included in this category.

(b) Larger private sector metalliferous and non-metalliferous mines.

(c) Small mines and quarries.[2]

The workers in the first category of mines are mostly employed directly by the enterprises though, on some jobs, contract labour is also engaged. In the second and third categories of mines, workers are mostly employed through contractors. Workers' organisations are fairly strong in the first category of mines. They are sufficiently active in the second category of mines as well. Workers in third category mines are mostly Unorganised. The working conditions of workers working in underground mines are full of hazards.[3]

The mines falling in the first category provide welfare measures for workers, such as healthcare, education of children and housing or house rent allowance. They also provide social security benefits in accordance with the social security laws and schemes. The second category of mines normally provides social security benefits as per social security laws, but other benefits such as healthcare or housing needs are not taken care of by the employers. In the third category of mines, workers do not have the benefit of any welfare measures. Employers normally try to avoid implementing social security laws and schemes in these mines by circumventing laws in various ways.[4]

Though *The Minimum Wages Act, 1948, The Equal Remuneration Act, 1976, The Contract Labour (R and A) Act, 1970, and the Interstate Migrant Workmen's (RE and CS) Act, 1979*, apply to the workers in these mines, we find that these laws are observed more in violation than in application. The incidence of child labour and bonded labour too is seen in quarries in gross violation of *the Mines Act, The Child Labour (P and R) Act, 1986,* and *Bonded Labour System Abolition Act, 1976.*

For example: Rajasthan has about 2 million mineworkers working throughout the State. 15% of them are children, and about 22,000 of them are in the age group of 10-12 years (60% of these children are bonded labourers). 37% of the total mineworkers are women, and more than 80% of all the mine-workers are in the age group of 16-40 years. Only 7% of mine workers are in the age group of above 40 years. Most of them become unfit for heavy work after 40 years of age.[5]

Working conditions in the mines are pathetic. There is no shade or protection for the mineworkers at the work place. They have to brave the harsh weather, scorching heat or chilled cold. Work in the mines is done manually with heavy hammers, chisels and other tools. Workers are exposed to serious health hazards, which affect their longevity.

2. PLANTATION WORKERS

The *Plantation Labour Act,* 1951 applies only to those plantations which measure 5 hectares or more, and in which 15 or more persons are employed or were employed on any day during the preceding 12 months. It includes workers employed in offices, hospitals, dispensaries, creches, balwadis and schools, but does not include those employed in a factory, medical officers or those employed in managerial capacity. It also does not apply to workers who get monthly wages of more than Rs. 750. The minimum wages received by a plantation worker in the Plantation industry in the South today vary between Rs. 59.02 – Rs. 81.75 per day, and in the North East, from Rs. 40 – Rs. 61.20 per day both of which are much higher than Rs. 750 per month. Thus legally, the situation that exists today is highly anomalous. No worker in any plantation is covered under the Act because the Act stipulates an upper wage limit of Rs. 750 per month.

Every plantation has a certain number of employees in its regular workforce. They are required for day to day jobs such as pruning, weeding, making roads and drains, planting and filling, spraying pest control chemicals, manuring, irrigation and other related jobs, including the manning of offices and administering, and overseeing welfare measures. A large number of additional workers are employed during the harvesting season for work such as plucking coffee beams or tapping rubber, or plucking cardamom pods, and peppers (plucking of tea leaves goes on almost round the year).[6]

Essentially, plantation operations have to be carried out in open fields. The workers are, therefore exposed to all the vagaries of climate and weather, such as scorching sun, heavy rain, and chilly winter, while at work. The Act stipulates that plantations employing 300 or more workers should provide the prescribed number of umbrellas, blankets, raincoats etc. for the protection of workers. To protect workers from insect bites, snakebites etc., it should be made mandatory for all employers to provide gumboots. It is also necessary to lay down safety norms in respect of the work of handling fertilisers and spraying pesticides. Other facilities like education, canteen and crèches, depend upon the number of workers employed.[7]

Workers, engaged on jobs other than harvesting of crops, are paid wages on time rate basis i.e. daily rates, while those engaged in harvesting are paid wages on the piece-rate system. For workers on the piece-rate system, there are incentive schemes too, if their output exceed fixed norms. In plantations in Southern India, wages, including payments of incentives, are decided by mutual negotiations, while in Assam wages are paid as notified by the State Government under *The Minimum Wages Act*. In Thiruvananthapuram and Guwahati the proper wages are not paid to contract workers as the middlemen keep their margin out of the wages given by the management. The National Commission on Labour, 2002 recommend that the State Governments, and the employers ensure that workers are paid proper wages as decided by settlements or notified under *the Minimum Wages Act*, and middlemen do not siphon away part of the wages that legitimately belong to the workers.

3. HOME WORKERS/HOME-BASED WORKERS

The home worker or home-based worker falls within a grey area, in a category between employed workers and self-employed workers. There is no system to enforce minimum wages because of the informal contractual relationship between the worker and the employer, the employer's agent or the contractor. Usually the home worker is looked upon as a self-employed person, and not a 'worker'. But, there are self-employed workers, as well as workers employed by others, among home-based workers. It has been pointed out that 'the term home-based workers' refers to two types of workers who carry out remunerative work within their homes : (a) independent own account producers, and (b) dependent subcontract workers-whereas the term 'home workers' refers only to the second category. Under this usage, home workers are a subset of home-based workers.[8]

The ILO Convention No. 177 of 1996 (Convention Concerning Home Work) clarifies that 'many International Labour Conventions and Recommendations laying down standards of general application concerning working conditions are applicable to home workers.'

Article 1 of the Convention No. 177 defines a home worker and an employer. In the eyes of this Convention Article 1 of this Convention says:

(a) the term 'home work' refers to the work carried out by a person, who is to be referred to as a home worker,

- in his, or her home, or in other premises of his or her choice, other than the workplace of the employer;
- for remuneration;
- that which result in a product or service as specified by the employer irrespective of who provides the equipment, materials or other inputs used, unless this person has the degree of autonomy and of economic independence necessary to be considered an independent worker under national laws, regulations or court decisions;

(b) persons with employee status do not become home workers within the meaning of this Convention simply by occasionally performing their work as employees at home, rather than at their usual workplaces;

(c) the term 'employer' means a person, natural or legal, who either directly or through an intermediary, whether or not intermediaries are provided for in national legislation, gives out home work in pursuance of his or her business activity.

The ILO definition, thus does not give importance to who provides the raw materials and inputs. It only refers to such factors as the dependency of the worker, his or her involvement in producing the product/rendering the services specified by the employer for remuneration, and the work being carried out at home or a place of the worker's choice.

A National Consultation with the Labour Secretaries, Labour Commissioners of the State Governments, representatives of Central Ministries and Departments, research and academic institutions, and NGOs/representatives of home-based workers was held on the 17th January 2000 in New Delhi. The discussion paper presented by the Ministry of Labour at the Consultation made an effort to define home-based workers. Paragraphs 4 to 12 of the paper try to explain the characteristics and situation of HBWs in India. The paper says: "Home based Workers are those who are otherwise unemployed, intending to, but not absorbed by the organised sector with skills limited to certain jobs which have economic value. . . ." The issues and problems of such workers are complicated, because of there being no direct employer-employee relationship between the home worker and the person or organisation for whom he works—the relationship being of a loose, contractual and tenuous nature. The relationship being ambiguous and indefinite, he is also subjected to exploitation in various forms. The home worker is, thus, a self-employed person conducting his economic activity for a person or an organisation. The mode of payment or price can be on piece-rate or time rate basis, depending on the economic activity.

4. DOMESTIC WORKERS

The Domestic workers are find in the urban areas as well as rural areas. It is well known that many persons; who are employed in domestic work, are people who have migrated to the urban areas in search of employment. It is believed that domestic service does not need any special skill. Perhaps those who seek such service are also under the impression that they will be protected in the household, and will receive the kind of treatment that can be expected from the members of a respectable family. There are many instances which show that they are extremely poor, illiterate, that they come from rural areas and have no acquaintance with the ways of the town and townspeople.[9]

They have to eke out their existence and therefore, often agree to work at nominal wages, taking the risks of uncertainty and uncivil or inhuman conditions of work and treatment. The existing law do not provide them the protection they need. It is well known that there is no system of social security on which they can fall back. In general, the circumstances are such that domestic workers have a very hard life. There are no fixed hours of work. In many cases they are not provided with adequate food. They do not earn enough to buy adequate clothing. Again, in many cases, they are not provided with a safe and clean place where they can rest and sleep. It is not said that all households in which domestic servants are employed treat their servants shabbily. There are many employers whose attitude is enlightened and who look upon those who work in their homes, as those who work with them, helping them with the daily chores in the house hold. In spite of all these, it can hardly be claimed that the domestic workers gets his/her hard earned dues, in terms of wages, limitation on hours of work, humane treatment, care in cases of illness, opportunity to enjoy leisure, medical needs and so on. It must be pointed out that since most of the domestic servants are women and children, they run the risk of sexual harassment and exploitation in some houses.[10]

It is therefore, very clear that domestic servants must be provided at least a modicum of protection and satisfactory safeguards for security. In Mumbai, during evidence sessions, Non-Governmental group has formulated a Bill that incorporates provisions for protection and safety of domestic workers. They wanted that any such law must provide for the benefits of PF, Gratuity, medical needs, leave, fixed working hours, wages and social security. The promoters of the Bill asked for the following:

(a) The domestic worker should be recognised as a worker, and issued an identity card or and letter of appointment.
(b) Working hours for domestic workers should be fixed at 8 hours a day.
(c) They should be paid overtime allowances in case they have to work longer.
(d) They must be entitled to some personal free time during the day.
(e) They should have access to the provision of PF and Gratuity, and be provided with uniforms.

The Bill provides for the appointment of an Advisory Body consisting of social workers, representatives of trade unions, and domestic workers. It also wants labour judiciary to be empowered to look into disputes between domestic workers and employers.

The National Commission on Labour, 2002 said that the proposals contained in the Bill are goals towards which we have to work. We strongly feel that adequate protection should be made to ensure satisfactory conditions of work, humane treatment and acceptable levels of social security. We are not proposing a separate piece of legislation to cover the domestic workers, primarily because we want to minimize the number of separate laws for different kinds of workers. Our attempt is to ensure that the existing laws are consolidated, and reformulated to provide protection and welfare, to all workers.

5. CONTRACT LABOUR

Unlike direct labour which is borne on the pay or muster roll of the establishment and entitled to be paid wages directly, contract labour by and large, is neither borne on pay-roll nor is paid directly. The establishment which farms out work to a contractors does not owe any direct responsibility in regard to his/their labour. In several contracts the wage rates to be paid to labour are stipulated, but whether payment is made on that basis or not is hardly the concern of the contractor himself or of the person/organisations for whom the contractor works.[11]

The advantages to the employer in employing contract labour are:

(i) production at lower cost;
(ii) engaging labour without having to extend fringe benefits such as leave wages, Employees' State Insurance or Provident Fund contributions and bonus;
(iii) general reduction of the overhead cost and the administrative burden of maintaining an establishment.

Contract labour can broadly be divided into two set categories; those employed on job contracts, and others on labour contracts. Large establishments give out contracts of jobs or of particular operations, e.g. loading and unloading, to contractors on lump-sum payment. The contractor engages his own workers. The contractor can be an individual or an establishment or even a senior worker like a maistry or a mukadam or a sirdar. The protection received by contract labour varies according to the situation.[12]

Section 2 (b) of *The Contract Labour (Regulation and Abolition) Act*, 1970 defined Contract Labour. A workmen shall be deemed to be employed as "contract labour" in or in connection with the work of an establishment when he is hired in or in connection with such work by or through a contractor, with or without the knowledge of principal employer.

In National Federation of Rly. Porters, Vendors and Bearers v. Union of India,[13] the Supreme Court on the basis of report of the Labour Commissioner to the effect that the petitioners have been working as parcel porters and all of them have completed more than 240 days of continuous service directed the petitioners to be absorbed permanently as regular Railway Parcel Porters of the stations where they were working as such.

Similarly in *T.N. Electricity Employees and Contract Labour Union v. T.N. Electricity Board,*[14] Supreme Court directed the absorption of all remaining workers and refused to give any further extension of time.

In *Air India Statutory Corporation v. United Labour Union.*[15] It was held that though there is no provision in *the Contract Labour (Regulation and Abolition) Act, 1970* for absorption of the employees whose contract labour system stood abolished under the Act. But the Act does not prohibit the corporation to absorb them in regular service and that is the mandate of the Constitution in Article-21. The contractor stands removed and direct relationship of employer and employee is created between the principal employer and workmen.

The Constitution Bench of the Supreme Court in *Steel Authority of India Ltd. v. National Union Water Front Workers*[16] ruled:

> Neither Section 10 of the CLRA Act nor any other provision in the Act, whether expressly or by necessary implication provides for automatic absorption of contract labour on issuing a notification by appropriate government under Sub-Section (1) of Section 10 prohibiting employment of contract labour, in any process, operation or other work in any establishment. Consequently, the principal employer cannot be required to order absorption of the contract labour working in the concerned establishment.

The Constitution Bench accordingly overruled the judgement in *Air India's case* prospectively thereby, *inter alia*, denied the right of contract labour to be absorbed, on abolition of contract labour system, a right earlier created by another three judge-bench by judicial legislation. However, the principles evolved in the SAIL judgement are pregnant with tremendous liability and would bring anomalous results.

The scope of the definition of "worker" in *The Factories Act, 1948, The Mines Act, 1952 and The Plantations Labour Act*, 1951 was enlarged to include contract labour. Contract labour in some sectors became entitled to the benefits of working conditions and hours of work admissible to the labour directly employed. The definition of the term "immediate employer" under *The Employees' State insurance Act, 1948* extended health insurance benefits to contract labour. The *Dock workers' (Regulation of Employment) Act, 1948* protected the employment, wages and welfare conditions of specified categories of contract labour employed at major docks. The provisions of *Minimum Wages Act, 1948* applied to contract labour in scheduled employment. The *Bombay Industrial Relations Act, 1946* and similar Acts in Madhya Pradesh and Uttar Pradesh cover contract labour. They are thus entitled in these States to bring up issues in dispute and enjoy protection and benefits as are available to directly employed workmen under the said Acts.

Occupations on which contract labour is employed range from purely unskilled work categories as loader, unloader, cleaner, sweeper and khalasi to skilled employment as polisher, turner, gas cutter and rivetter in oil distribution and driller, blaster, blacksmith, carpenter and fitter in the mining industry. Apart from these, there are certain regular processes such as nickel polishing and electro-plating in engineering establishments, dyeing, bleaching and printing in some units in textiles, and designing and 'raising' work in almost all carpet in manufacturing units, where contract labour is common.

Contract labour is generally paid wages below the rates prescribed for regular workers in the industry. Often they do not get any payment other than the basic remuneration. Conditions of work are also far from satisfactory. Working hours are irregular and longer. The period for which payment is made varies from a day to six months. There is no security of employment; the job ends with the contract.

With a view to removing the disabilities of contract labour, *Contract Labour (Regulation and Abolition) Act, 1970*, has been passed. It provides for (i) the registration of principal employers and licensing of contractors, (ii) the regulation of conditions of work, payment of minimum wages, and other essential amenities relating to welfare and health of contract labour, and (iii) a comprehensive definition of the terms 'work', 'principal employer' and 'workmen'.

6. CONSTRUCTION LABOUR

Construction workers may be broadly classified as skilled and unskilled. Though child labour is prohibited, children are engaged for unskilled jobs. Most of the workers in this sector are employed on a casual basis. Unstable employment/earnings and shifting of workplaces are the basic characteristics of work for constructions workers. Employment in construction is usually interspersed with periods of unemployment of varying duration, mainly due to fluctuating requirements of labour force on each worksite. The nature of work is such that there are no holidays. It is established that female workers do not in general get minimum wages. Though skilled workers secure jobs directly from employers, unskilled workers by and large, are engaged through intermediaries who introduce the workers to contractors on a commission basis.[17]

Since workers are generally recruited on contract basis, failing to achieve the required quantum of work results in either deductions or uncompensated overtime work. In return for providing jobs, the intermediaries often collect commission from each worker at a fixed rate for each working day. Women engaged in construction work, are the most exploited. What is worse, the contractors remove sick and injured workers from sites and pay rolls without giving them adequate compensation.

Unorganised construction workers can truly be described as sweat labour, and violation of laws on minimum wages, equal wages, child labour, contract labour, interstate migrant workers etc. is rampant in construction as in agriculture and home-based occupations. Unionisation is not allowed or encouraged, and construction workers like many others in the Unorganised sector remain invisible and vulnerable voiceless and un-unionised.[18]

The existing labour laws applicable to construction workers are based on inspection, prosecution, fines, etc. However, legal processes are so time consuming that the aggrieved worker may be out of employment or employed elsewhere by the time redressal materializes. He/She cannot leave his/her worksite, forgoing his/her daily wages to go elsewhere to pursue complaints against violation of laws. The existing laws do not give adequate protection to workers against victimisation.

Unskilled and semiskilled workers have no option in regard to their working hours. They have to do what the mistri asks them to do. In excavation, earthwork, stone breaking and stone and marble dressing, the work unit is generally, the family or the gang, and they normally work 12 hours a day; all seven days of the week.

The social safety network of building workers is built around kinship and tradition, and trade unions have not yet found a place in this system. Contractors are paternalistic, their style of management may be authoritarian. A contractor may be tight-fisted in fixing rates of payment and may not spend on latrines, urinals and other facilities at worksites. But he would be generous when a worker sought help from him for celebrating his daughter's marriage, attending to illness in the family etc.[19]

One of the statutory obligation of a contractor is that he should provide workers, at his own cost, with living accommodation of given specifications. In so far as the quantitative compliance of the statutes was concerned, contractors had met their obligation of providing residential accommodation to workers. Of 999 respondents, 825 had been provided accommodation by contractors. All respondents who lived at worksites used community toilet facilities, drew water from site sources and depended upon site lamp-posts for lighting.[20]

7. BIDI WORKERS

Employment in tobacco processing, including bidi manufactories, is included in the Schedule to *The Minimum Wages Act, 1948*. According to 1961 Census there were nine lakhs of workers engaged in the industry, of whom about 5.5 lakhs were in the household sector. In 1964-65, the number of registered trade unions in tobacco manufactories was 1811 with a membership of 97,000. Working conditions prevailing in the bidi and cigar establishments have been unsatisfactory for the reason that although the labour laws, like *The Factories Act, 1948* apply to such establishments, some employers, particularly bigger ones, circumvent the provisions of the Act by splitting their concerns into smaller units. Most of these units are ill ventilated and workers are crowded in dark and dingy rooms. There are also no fixed hours of work of any permanency benefits for workers; victimisation in small units is common.[21]

Apart from workshop or factory system of production, manufacture of bidis is organised through contractors or by distributing work in private dwellings where workers take raw materials given by the employer or his contractor and hand over the finished product at the stipulated place. The system of payment in the bidi industry is mainly on piece-rate basis, except in the case of workers like wrappers, labellers, and sorters who are normally employed on a monthly basis. Deductions from wages in the industry are frequent and on various counts. Wages are deducted for preparation of substandard bidis and misuse of leaves or tobacco. A complaint voiced by workers was that no payment is made for rejected bidis.[22]

The profit margin in the bidi industry can be lucrative when the brand is established in the market. With modern salesmanship entering the bidi industry, it is brand which sells and this makes it difficult for newcomers to enter the industry. Since the employer-employee relationship is not well defined, the application of *The Factories Act* has run into difficulties in this industry as in other small scale units. Some State Governments have passed special laws to regulate the conditions of work in bidi establishments but are unable to enforce the law owing to mobility of the industry. The Central Government has, therefore, enacted *The Bidi and Cigar Workers (Conditions of Employment) Act, 1966* to regulate the system of work and licensing of premises on which the manufacture of bidi and cigar is carried on, and also to deal with matters such as health, hours of work, spread over and annual leave.[23]

One of the ways in which workers in this industry can get relief is through organisatioin of co-operatives. Attempts made in this direction have not yielded results so far.

8. TRIBAL LABOUR

Tribal labour as an ethnic group is relatively cohesive sensitive to changes which appear to its imagination to be almost revolutionary particularly as taking place in its homelands. Since independence, large scale industries have been set up in the areas the peace of which had not been disturbed over ages. The process of industrialisation has made a vital impact on the tribal economy and its social structure, which are disintegrating. The Study Group on Tribal Labour has observed that it will be a great loss for development if tribal people are not helped, given time to undergo this cultural mutation and to work out for themselves a synthesis of traditional and modern culture. Large industrial undertakings cannot exist as islands in tribal areas: these have to be integrated with the life of the tribal people at some points. There is thus the need for a basic change in employment policy towards tribal labour, which merely thought in terms of reservation of certain percentage of posts. New dimensions to this policy will be formulation of programmes for recruitment, training and promotion, all of which need to be reviewed and re-assessed from the point of view of actual benefits and effects they produce on tribal labour. Tribals have demanded certain privileges and rights and opportunities as 'sons of the soils': these demands cannot be brushed aside, because the tribals have lost their lands which have been acquired for development and have suffered on many counts to facilitate industrial undertakings to come up.[24]

Steps should be taken to ensure that local tribal labour, especially the displaced labour, gets reasonable opportunity for recruitment to unskilled and semi-skilled jobs. It should be the duty of the management to arrange for training and education of these workers for skilled positions when employment opportunities are created or are available.[25]

9. CASUAL LABOUR

The incidence of casual labour is determined by the nature of the task to be performed. Employment of casual labour is a common feature in the Railways, the Public Works Departments, both Central and State, the State Electricity Corporations and employments in the private sector where the nature of work is similar.[26]

Employment of casual labour in several categories of work is well recognised and not objected to. It is taken exception to mainly when such labour continually employed for long periods to circumvent the provisions of law, which confer benefits to permanent workers through better working conditions, more amenities, and the like, and what is more, when used deliberately to restrict the scope for regular employment. Though de-casualisation has made some headway in State Government Departments, Railways and Ports and Docks and some industrial centres where several units of the same industry operate, there is still a large volume of casual labour which is engaged for varying lengths of time; not in all cases are they kept casual for bona fide reasons.[27]

Though casual labour comes under the scope of some labour enactments relating to wages and regulation of hours of work and conditions of service, it is deprived of the advantages accruing from legislation which stipulates continuous employment for being elegible. Casual labour is thus denied annual leave with wages, maternity and sickness benefits because under the law a worker must complete a minimum period of work in an establishment as a pre-condition for eligibility.[28]

Casual labour should be restricted to work which is truly of a casual nature and it should be employed only where regular workers cannot be employed. For this purpose, every enterprise should determine well in advance the strength of labour force, both permanent and temporary, in consultation with representatives of labour. Wherever possible there should be a standing order which should, against the 'normal' strength of the enterprise concerned, fix the strength of casual labour. *The National Commission on Labour, 1969* consider the prevailing practice of discontinuing employment of a causal worker for short periods and again re-employing him to debar him from enjoying the benefits of a permanent worker as pernicious and recommehd that if employment is discontinued for a short period and the worker is re-employed, this short period should not be treated as a break in service.[29]

10. SCAVENGERS

There is a very large number of people-engaged in manual scavenging in different parts of the country, in rural areas as well as urban areas. Allocation of labour on the basis of caste is one of the fundamental tenets of the caste system. Within the caste system, Dalits have been assigned tasks and occupations that are deemed virtually polluting for other caste communities. Throughout this report, Human Rights watch has documented the exploitation of agricultural labourers who work for a few kilograms of rice or Rs. 15 to Rs. 35 a day. An estimated forty million people in India, among them fifteen million children, are bonded labourers. A majority of them are Dalits. According to Government statistics, an estimated one million Dalits are manual scavengers who clean public latrines and dispose off dead animals, unofficial estimates are much higher. Scavenging is the hereditary occupation of some 'untouchable' castes. Dalits face discrimination when seeking other forms of employment, and are largely unable to escape their designated occupation even when the practice has been abolished by law.[30]

Manual scavenging has been a caste-based occupation. Dalit manual scavengers exist under different caste names throughout the country, such as the Bhangis in Gujarat, the Pakhis in Andhra Pradesh, and the Sikkaliars in Tamil Nadu. Members of these communities are invariably placed at the very bottom of the caste hierarchy, and even the hierarchy of Dalit sub-castes. Though outlawed, the practice of manual scavenging continues in most states.[31]

In a 1997 report, *The National Commission for Safai Karamcharis* claimed that manual scavengers are 'totally cut off from the mainstream of progress' and are still subjected to the worst kind of oppression and indignities. *Safai Karamcharis* are defined as persons engaged in, or employed for, manually carrying human excreta or any sanitation work.

Martin Macwan is founder-director of Navsarjan, an NGO that has led the compaign to abolish manual scavenging in the Western State of Gujarat. In an interview with Human Rights Watch, he claimed that when Navsarjan attempted to rehabilitate scavengers it was difficult to convince scavengers that they were able to take on, or were 'worthy of performing', different occupations.

Social discrimination against scavengers is rampant. Most scavengers live in segregated rural colonies and are unable to make use of common resources.

The Employment of Manual Scavengers and Construction of Dry Latrines (Prohibition) Act, 1993 punishes the employment of scavengers or the construction of dry (non-flush) latrines with imprisonment for up to one year and/or a fine as high as Rs. 2,000. 212 offenders are also liable to prosecution under *The Scheduled Castes and Scheduled Tribes (Prevention of Atrocities) Act, 1989*. In 1992 the Government launched a National Scheme that called for the identification, training, and rehabilitation of safai karamcharis throughout the country.

According to *The National Commission for Safai Karamcharis,* the progress 'has not been altogether satisfactory'. As a result, it has benefited only 'a handful of safai karamcharis and their dependents. One of the reason for unsatisfactory progress of the scheme appears to be inadequate attention paid to it by the State Governments and concerned agencies.'

11. RAG PICKERS

Rag picking and other scrap collection are not a new phenomenon especially in industrial towns and metropolitan cities. They have a bearing on the urban economy. Many production enterprises depend upon the recycling of these wastes. Scrap collection is mostly done by women and children in a working environment that is most unhygienic.[32]

According to available estimates, there are about 50 lakh scrap collectors in the country. The number is far greater if labourers in scrap establishments and re-processing units are included. Illiterates, unskilled persons, illegal aliens and the poorest of the poor are pushed into this occupation, as they are unable to find any other kind of employment. Generally, there is no employer-employee relationship in this trade even though it is possible that some of the scrap picking activity is organised by contractors. Waste collectors are generally categorished as self-employed. Scrap collectors are not covered under *The Shops and Establishment Act,* as scrap traders do not provide any kind of receipts to them for the material they collect. No social security benefits are available to worker in this sector.[33]

During visit to pune, *The Kagad Kanch Patra Kashtkari Panchayat,* which is a trade union of scrap collectors, told about the issues and problems that affect scrap collectors. There are about 5,000 waste pickers and waste collectors in Pune who are registered with this trade union. There are over one lakh persons engaged in waste picking and others forms of scrap collection in the urban areas of the State of Maharasthra. The demands put by the union were:

(a) It must be mandatory for all municipalities to register wastepickers and other scrap collectors, and to issue a photo identity card to each such worker as has been done by the Pune and Pimpri Chinchwad Municipal Corporations.

(b) Scrap collectors should be registered as unprotected manual workers under the Mathadi Board constituted under *The Maharashtra Hamal Mathadi and other Unprotected Manual Workers (Regulation of Employment and Welfare) Act, 1969.* Similarly it should be mandatory for all scrap traders and/or recycling enterprises to be registered under the same Act. It should be mandatory for the scrap traders and/or recycling enterprises to contribute the applicable levy towards the contributory provident fund, gratuity, paid leave, insurance and other statutory benefits as provided for under the Act.

(c) It should be mandatory for all municipalities to earmark green zones in each ward where waste-pickers can sit and sort their scrap.

(d) It should be mandatory for the municipalities to provide a rest room, drinking water, toilet and creche facilities at garbage dumping grounds/landfill sites.

(e) All registered scrap collectors should be listed as falling below the Urban Poverty Line by the municipalities for the purposes of State Social Security Schemes for the weaker sections.

(f) Child labour should not be permitted in waste picking. Waste picking should be included in the schedule of prohibited hazardous occupations under *The Child Labour (Prohibition and Regulation) Act, 1986.*

A study of scrap collectors/scrap traders and recycling enterprises in Pune has been conducted by the United Nations Development Programme and International Labour Organisation. The main objectives of the study were to assess the socio-economic conditions of these workers, to identify the variables to improve their living and working conditions, and explore the possibilities of extending available legislations for their protection, etc.

The study shows that about 92% of scrap collectors are women in the age group of 19 to 50. The mean age of entry of those who entered this occupation is 9-10 years. The mean monthly per capita income of scrap collector's family ranges between Rs. 126 to Rs. 2,233. They are also victims of harassment from police or municipal officials.

The study made the following recommendations:

(a) Scrap collectors should be recognised as 'unprotected manual workers' who contribute to the economy and the environment in significant ways.
(b) The conditions of work of scrap collectors, particularly waste pickers are 'abominable'. Widespread and intensive compaigning should be undertaken to educate citizens about the advantages in segregation of garbage, and direct access to waste pickers should be mandated by the local self-Government.
(c) Child labour in scrap collection is hazardous, and should be included in the schedule of Hazardous occupations as listed in *The Child Labour (Prohibition and Regulation) Act.*

The Commission recognises the useful role played by the scrap collectors both in helping recycling activities as well as in maintaining civic hygiene. It is, therefore, essential that they should be protected from insecurity of various forms. The measures that could be thought of in this regard are providing identity cards, receipts for transactions, minimum wages when they are employed by contractors or other employers, health facilities, creation of welfare funds, prohibition of child labour from the activity and the like.

12. STREET VENDORS

Street vendors and hawkers are among the most visible and active category of the workforce in the informal sector. Most of them come from impoverished rural families. Street vending absorbs millions of those who come to cities as economic refugees from the villages, because they can enter this occupation with small amounts of capital. They not only create employment for themselves through their entrepreneurial skills, but also generate upstream employment in agriculture as well a small-scale industry. They are the main distribution channel for a large variety of products of daily consumption-fruit, vegetables, readymade garments, stationery, newspapers, magazines and so on. Their elimination from urban markets would lead to a severe crisis for fruit and vegetable farmers, as well as small-scale industries which cannot afford to retail their products through expensive distribution networks in the formal sector.[34]

The activities of hawkers and street vendors are comprehensive and ingenuous. There are hawkers in Delhi who collect dal and spices which spill on the road during transportation, clean them and sell them to the poorer sections of the population. There are hawkers in Chennai who have set up a whole market for imported electronic consumer goods. A large section of population in all cities is dependent on vendors and hawkers for their meals and snacks.[35]

Laws relating to street vending are varied. With the exception of Kolkata, most municipalities have provisions for providing licenses for hawking. Kolkata not only considers street vending an illegal activity, but its law provides very stringent punishment for hawkers: hawking is a cognisable and non-bailable offence.

Imphal is one city which has clearly laid down rules for street vending. *The Manipur Town Planning and Country Planning Act, 1975,* provides that in residential areas there should be a provision for 4 to 6 shops and 10 hawkers per 1000 people.

The fact that street vending is looked upon as a nuisance or frowned upon by law gives a lever to the municipal authorities and police to extort money from the vendors. Municipalities should seriously think of alternative solutions. Legalizing vending by providing licenses may solve many of the problems that are being faced today. Bribery and corruption will decrease, municipalities will earn more through license fees, and street vending will get more orderly, disciplined and regulated.

Most countries in the developing world are facing problems in identifying to role of vendors and providing a framework that enables them to make their contribution to the economy, employment generation, and the services sector. This is evident by the declaration that was adopted at *The*

International Conference on Vendors that was organised at the initiative of SEWA and other similar organisations at Bellagio in 1995.

The Bellagio International Declaration of Street Vendors adopted on November 23, 1995 says:

'Having Regard to the Fact':

(a) That because of poverty, unemployment and forced migration and immigration, despite the useful service they render to society, they are looked upon as an hindrance to the planned development of cities both by the elite urbanites and the town planners alike;

(b) That hawkers and vendors are subjected to constant mental and physical torture by the local officials and are harassed in many other ways which at times leads to riotous situation, loss of property rights, or monetary loss; and

(c) That there is hardly any public police consistent with the needs of street vendors throughout the world.

'We urge upon Governments:

(a) To form a National Policy for hawkers and vendors by making them a part of the broader structural policies aimed at improving their standards of living, by having regard to the following;

(b) Give vendors legal status by issuing licenses, enacting laws and providing appropriate hawking zones in urban plans; and

(c) Protect and expand vendors' existing livelihood.

13. RICKSHAW PULLERS

Rickshaw pullers, particularly in the North, are mostly migrants. They migrate from the States of Bihar, Orissa, Madhya Pradesh, Uttar Pradesh and Rajasthan to bigger towns and cities. Most of them are small are peasants or landless the cities due to feudal oppression, exploitation by land mafia, or natural calamities like recurring floods. In big towns they have no place to stay. They generally sleep on footpaths or in their rickshaws.

All of them do not own rickshaws. They take them on hire, and have to pay a large sum of money as rent, even if they do not earn enough. Often, they are harassed by the police. They do not have any social security cover.[36]

Rickshaw pullers are among the least protected workers in the unorganised sector. Conditions are not regulated. Nor are their social security issues addressed. The vulnerability of rickshaw pullers is further accentuated by the fact that the majority of those who pull rickshaws do not own the rickshaw themselves. In a city like Delhi, only 14.6% rickshaw are licensed. The rules of the Municipal Corporation permit only one rickshaw for one person. They also stipulate that the owner himself has to be the puller. Illegal ownership and unlicensed plying add to the complexity of the conditions in the sector.[37]

The life of a rickshaw puller is not, however easy. The nature of the work itself has a number of hardships built into it. It is hard work further aggravated by the badly maintained roads. The rickshaw puller has to work in the open and, therefore, is at the mercy of nature. Most of the rickshaw pullers are migrants, and generally stay alone in the urban areas while their families live in the villages. The rickshaw puller has to save some money to send it home to take care of his family. Most of the rickshaw pullers just manage to earn their livelihood. Their earnings range from Rs. 40 per day to Rs. 150 per day depending upon the city in which they operate and the season.

Most of them smoke beedis, chew tobacco and quite a number of them drink locally brewed alcohol. The cumulative effect of this style is that a large number of rickshaw pullers, especially in the smaller cities, suffer from tuberculosis and other diseases. Since there is no medical scheme for these persons, disease tend to aggravate.

Apart from providing direct employment to lakhs of persons, rickshaw pulling provides indirect employment to several others due to its multiplier effect. The rickshaw manufacturing activity and rickshaw repair activity perhaps give employment to a number of persons. If we take into account the fact that each such person looks after 5-6 members of his family, it would imply that the rickshaw pullers sustain a large section of the population and this, at a time when the organised sector is not in a position to offer any jobs.

The Prime Minister recently intervened to help the rickshaw pullers of Delhi and wrote to the Lt. Governor of Delhi stressing 'it policy should recognize street hawking and cycle rickshaw pulling as legitimate occupations which help reduce poverty and facilitate their integration into the formal economy.' The note from the PMO highlighted the following issues:

(i) Existing license system with quantitative limits must be scrapped.

(ii) The metropolis must be divided into green, amber and the red zones signifying free access, fee based access and prohibited access respectively.

Any person who wishes to be a street hawker or cycle rickshaw puller may do so by a simple act of registration. The sole purpose of registration would be to provide identification.[38]

14. AGRICULTURAL WORKERS, MARGINAL FARMERS AND SHARECROPPERS

The Annual Report of the Ministry of Labour, 1999-2000 considers cultivators, sharecroppers and agricultural labourers as unorganised workers. In fact, the agricultural sector constitutes the largest segment of workers in the unorganised sector. Inadequacy of employment opportunities, poor security of tenure, low incomes, and inadequate diversification of economic activities are the main problems for the workers in this sector. Agricultural labour gets employment for less than six months in the year, and they have often to migrate to other avenues of employment, like construction and similar occupations during the off-season. Circumstances force most agricultural workers to borrow money from time to time from private sources, either for needs of consumption or for meeting social obligations like marriages.

It is estimated that out of 369 millions workers in the unorganised sector, 237 million workers are in activities that relate to agriculture. Agricultural labourers constitute a distinct section in the peasantry. Yet, their total strength, community allegiance, comparative socio-economic status and political position in agrarian society have been overlooked because they belong to a poorly organised, badly exploited and oppressed class of rural society. They are unable to organise themselves despite being a distinct class, because they are absolutely dependent on landowners. They often treat their agricultural labour as slaves, and pay wages in kind.[39]

Since agricultural workers are unorganised, their bargaining capacity is marginal; this leads to ruthless exploitation by moneylenders, and rich farmers. The report of *The National Commission on Rural Labour* has made observations on the acute indebtedness of rural workers and agricultural labour households. It observed that about 16.08 million rural labour households, including those of agricultural labour, were indebted. Of these, 5.67 million were from Scheduled Tribes. 8.62 millions were others.

A majority of agricultural workers had to seek loans to meet their basic needs. This clearly shows that agricultural workers did not receive the minimum wages prescribed by the States. It has been observed that approximately 40% of agricultural workers are migrant labourers. The migration ranges from inter-district migration to inter-state migration, and even migration to far off States like workers from Bihar migrating to Punjab and U.P., and workers from Chattisgarh migrating to Maharashtra, Gujarat and Punjab. The problems of all migrant workers are very severe. Most of them work for 12 hours a day; they do not get weekly rest. There is very scanty availability of housing or dwelling units. *The Inter-State Migrant Workmen's Act, 1979* has proved ineffective because of the reluctance of State Labour Departments to cooperate with the Labour Departments of the originating State, ineffective enforcement and the ignorance of agricultural workers. It is admitted that the agriculture of many prosperous State like Punjab depends on the labour of migrant workers. These States owe their prosperity to migrant workers, and it is therefore legitimate to demand that migrant workers should receive commensurately fair treatment, to assure them fair housing, adequate wages, social security and similar benefits.

The existing labour laws which are applicable to, and partially safeguard the interest of agricultural workers are: *(i) The Workmen's Compensation Act, 1923; (ii) The Minimum*

Wages Act, 1948; (iii) The Maternity Benefit Act, 1961; (iv) Contract Labour (Regulation and Abolition) Act, 1970; (v) The Personal Injuries (Compensation Insurance) Act, 1973; (vi) The Bonded Labour System (Abolition) Act, 1976; (vii) The Inter-State Migrant Workmen (RE and CS) Act, 1979; (vii) The Child Labour (Prohibition and Regulation) Act, 1986 and; (IX) Payment of Wages Act, 1936. The legislation dealing with aspect of safety is: *(i) Insecticides Act, 1968, and (ii) Dangerous Machines (Regulation) Act, 1983.* The Government also implements several schemes and programmes for the welfare of rural workers including agricultural workers such as *The Employment Assurance Scheme, Jawahar Gram Samridhi Yojana, Swarnajayanti Gram Swarojgar Yojana,* etc. However, considering the inadequacy of these legislative measures and welfare schemes, attempts have been made to enact a separate comprehensive legislation for agricultural workers. A draft Bill, *'The Agricultural Workers (Employment, Conditions of Service and Welfare Measures), Bill, 1997'* was prepared by the Central Government. However, the efforts of the Central Government have not succeeded so far because of opposition from some States that were opposed to Central legislation, and wanted the States to be left free to deal with the question, at a time, and in a way that they considered appropriate.

An agricultural worker has often been defined in Government statements as 'a person who follows one or more of the following agricultural occupations either as a smaller marginal land holder who part of the time offers himself for wage employment or a landlers labourer who offers himself for wage employment or a landless labourer who offer himself full time on hire, whether he is paid in cash or kind or partly in cash and partly in kind in any of the following activities: (a) farming, (b) dairy farming, (c) production, cultivation, growing and harvesting of any horticultural commodity, (d) raising of livestock, bee keeping or poultry farming, (e) fishing and, (f) any practice performed on a farm as incidental to or in conjunction with the farm operation and any forestry timbering operations and the preparation for market and delivery to storage or to market or to carriage for transportation of farm products.'

Unlike workers in the organised sector, agricultural workers do not have access to a system of social security or laws that provide for security of jobs, adequate minimum wages, and healthy and safe working conditions. They are the most vulnerable victims of natural calamities like floods or drought. They need protection from such disasters.

We have neglected the agricultural sector of the economy and agricultural labour during the last 50 years, although agriculture has been the backbone of our society and economy. It still holds the promise of prosperity. It is time that an effective framework of laws and social security was put in place for workers in this unorganised sector.

15. BONDED LABOUR

'Where a person provides labour or service to another for remuneration which is less than the minimum wage, the labour or service provided by him clearly falls within the scope and ambit of the words 'forced labour' under Article 23. The word 'force' must therefore be construed to include not only physical or legal force, but also force arising from the compulsion of economic circumstances which leaves no choice of alternatives to a person in want and compels him to provide labour or service even though the remuneration received for it is less than the minimum wage.'

The Bonded Labour System (Abolition) Act, 1976 and The Asiad Worker's case (People's Union for Democratic Rights v. Union of India[40]*)* together point out that the prevailing situation in some sub-sectors of the unorganised sector is equivalent to bondedness.

Section 2 of *The Bonded Labour System (Abolition) Act, 1976* defines the 'bonded labour system' as the system of forced, or partly forced labour, under which a debtor enters, or has, or is presumed to have, entered, into an agreement with the creditor to the effect that:

(a) in consideration of an advance obtained by him or by any of his lineal ascendants or descendants (whether or not such advance is evidence by any document) and in consideration of the interest, if any, due on such advance, or
(b) in pursuance of any customary or social obligation, or

(c) in pursuance of an obligation developing on him by succession, or
(d) for any economic consideration received by him or by any of his lineal ascendants or descendants, or
(e) by reason of his birth in any particular caste or community, he would:

- render, by himself or through any member of his family, or any person dependent on him, labour or service to the creditor, or for the benefit of the creditor, for a specified period or for an unspecified period, either without wages or for nominal wages, or
- forfeit the freedom of employment or other means of livelihood for a specified period or for an unspecified period, or
- forfeit the right to move freely throughout the territory of India, or
- forfeit the right to appropriate or sell at market value any of his property or product of his labour or the labour of a member of his family or any person dependent on him, and includes the system of forced, or partly forced, labour under which a surety for, a debtor enters, or has or is presumed to have, entered into an agreement with the creditor to the effect that in the event of the failure of the debtor to repay the debt, he would render the bonded labour on behalf of the debtor.

Article 23(1) of the Constitution of India, relating to fundamental rights, states that "traffic in human being and begar and other similar forms of forced labour are prohibited and any contravention of this provision shall be on offence punishable in accordance with law." The Hon'ble Supreme Court in *the People's Union for Democratic Rights* v. *Union of India*[41] *and Bandhu Mukti Morcha* v. *Union of India*[42] cases have redefined the scope of *the Bonded Labour System (Abolition) Act, 1976.*

In the *Asiad Workers' case,*[43] the Supreme Court pointed out that the Constitution makers decided "to give teeth to their resolve to obliterate and wipe out this evil practice by enacting constitutional prohibition against it in the chapter on Fundamental Rights, so that the abolition of such practice may become enforceable and effective as soon as the Constitution come into force."

The Asiad Workers' case added a very important dimension to the definition of bonded labour, when the Hon'ble Supreme Court ruled that force arising out of economic compulsions to make one volunteer to work below minimum wages, is also forced labour. The Court, basing its argument on Article 23, held that: 'This Act strikes at every form of forced labour even if it has its origin in a contract voluntarily entered into by the person obliged to provide labour or service. The reason is that it offends against human dignity to compel a person to provide labour or service to another if he does not wish to do so, even though it be in breach of the contract entered into by him.'

In *The Bandhua Mukti Morcha case,*[44] the power of the Supreme Court under Article 32 was invoked to free forced labour in two stone quarries in Faridabad. In the light of these historic judgements, when a person enters even into a willing contract by force of circumstances, if the person is paid only nominal wages or gets only nominal prices for products, the condition of the wage attract the rigour of the interpretation that the Supreme Court gave to Article 23. Therefore, the cases of farmers who do not get minimum prices for crops and workers who do not get minimum wages, need a correctional legislative step. In other words, both employed and self-employed workers need a guaranteed income or wage. Such a wage can be provided only through a comprehensive legislation on a National Minimum Wage.

16. OTHER COMMON PROPERTY RESOURCES-BASED WORKERS

Traditional artisans such as basket weavers and rope makers depend on a number of resources taken from forests and village commons. Village forests offer various varieties of grasses, canes and bamboo. The *'bann'* workers of Saharanpur produce ropes form the bhabhar grass, abundant in the Shivalik hills of Saharanpur district of Uttar Pradesh. Village commons are the source of food, fodder and fuel for the poor villagers.[45]

All these workers depending on common property

resources, whether employed or self-employed, have low earnings for a number of reasons such as depletion of resources and lack of work. Debt bondage is prevalent among them. It is obvious that they belong to the unorganised sector.[46]

Artisans: Artisans are persons with some skill or craft with which they produce products of every day use, ornamental goods or other tools for their livelihood. Like the home-based workers, some among the artisans are self-employed while some are employed under others. As in many cases raw materials are supplied, the products become linked, and a sort of chain gets established. For employed artisans as well as the self-employed artisans, wages and earnings are low.[47]

Unskilled Workers: Manual workers and a number of other workers in the unorganised sector performing diverse activities are considered unskilled workers. As specific skills are acquired through formal or informal training, untrained hands performing all kinds of jobs that do not need substantial specialization are treated as unskilled workers. Unskilled workers who are not employed in the organised sector, come in the category of workers in the unorganised sector. The majority of agricultural workers and construction workers belong to this category. Helper category of jobs in all sectors, the manual workers, roadside workers available for all kind of petty jobs, head load workers/porters, etc come under this category. It should be noted that they possess some skills that other persons in the skilled categories do not have. But since their wages are fixed low, these unorganised workers get only subsistence wages.[48]

Piece-rate Workers: Piece-rate workers do not constitute a separate category of employment, but consists of workers who are paid on a per-piece basis. The piece-rate issue is an extremely important, but has not been adequately addressed. Piece-rates are rampant in the unorganised sector. Many among the home based workers, contract workers, earth diggers, brick workers, etc. fall in this category. Piece rates are fixed in such a way that the wages earned are very low.[49] *The Minimum Wages Act, 1948* has provisions for both time-rates and piece-rates. But the mechanism for fixing piece-rates is not clearly spelt out. The Act also has provision for a 'guaranteed time-rate' for piecework.[50] But we find that this section has not been invoked adequately.

Unorganised Workers in the Organised Sector: Casual and contract workers in the organised sector are more or less equal to unorganised workers as far as benefits are concerned, through they are eligible for most of the benefits under law. Regular and permanent workers are mostly eligible for and receive legislative benefits. There is a section of workers on the official waitlist in most of the enterprises. They are the casual workers who are often called badli workers, daily wage workers and so on. The present trend is one of increasing casualisation where even regular workers in the organised sector are losing their work security. This section of labour, even though in the organised sector, has to be consider part of the unorganised sector. This is also the case with contract workers. Public sector undertaking engage contract labour. Often, these contract workers are not properly educated, not fully trained to handle machines, chemicals, electricity etc. Yet, they are employed to work on dangerous machines and dangerous processes. Contractualised and casualised labour has to be considered part of the unorganised sector.[51]

Notes and References

1. Mines Act, 1952, Section 2 (j).
2. Report of the Second National Commission on Labour, 2002, 7.69.
3. *Ibid.*, 2002, 7.69.
4. *Ibid.*, 2002, 7.72.
5. *Ibid.*, 2002, 7.73.
6. *Ibid.*, 2002, 7.60.
7. *Ibid.*, 2002, 7.61.
8. *Ibid.*, 2002, 7.33.
9. *Ibid.*, 2002, 7.48.
10. *Ibid.*, 2002, 7.49.
11. Report of the First National Commission on Labour, 1969, 29.4.
12. *Ibid.*, 1969, 29.5.
13. 1995 SCC (L and S), 1119.
14. *Ibid.*, 1130.
15. AIR 1997 SC 645.
16. 2001 LLR 961.
17. Report of the Second National Commission on Labour, 2002, 7.110.
18. *Ibid.*, 2002, 7.113.
19. *Ibid.*, 2002, 7.121.
20. *Ibid.*, 2002, 7.122.
21. Report of the First National Commission on Labour, 1969, 29.44.
22. *Ibid.*, 1969, 29.45.

23. *Ibid.*, 1969, 29.46.
24. *Ibid.*, 1969, 29.66.
25. *Ibid.*, 1969, 29.67.
26. *Ibid.*, 1969, 29 24.
27. *Ibid.*, 1969, 29.25.
28. *Ibid.*, 1969, 29.26.
29. *Ibid.*, 1969, 29.29.
30. Report of the Second National Commission on Labour, 2002, 7.77 to 7.79.
31. *Ibid.*, 2002, 7.80.
32. *Ibid.*, 2002, 7.127.
33. *Ibid.*, 2002, 7.128.
34. *Ibid.*, 2002, 7.223.
35. *Ibid.*, 2002, 7.224.
36. *Ibid.*, 2002, 7.240.
37. *Ibid.*, 2002, 7.243.
38. *Ibid.*, 2002, 7.253.
39. *Ibid.*, 2002, 7.269.
40. AIR 1982 SC, 1473.
41. *Ibid.*, 1473.
42. AIR 1984 SC, 802.
43. AIR 1982 SC, 1473.
44. *Ibid.*, SC, 802.
45. Report of the Second National Commission on Labour, 2002, 7.262.
46. *Ibid.*, 2002, 7.263.
47. *Ibid.*, 2002, 7.264.
48. *Ibid.*, 2002, 7.265.
49. *Ibid.*, 2002, 7.266.
50. The Minimum Wages Act, 1948, Section 3(2)(c).
51. Report of the Second National Commission on Labour, 2002, 7.267.

3

Labour Welfare Activities

Labour welfare is an extension of the term welfare and its application to labour. It is true that labour occupies an important position in every society, but its import has not always received the requisite accredition. If we examine the labour welfare services as organised by industry and talk to the personnel responsible for their maintenance, we note quite contradictory positions. In India, labour welfare started in its broader meaning, but has gradually become narrower in its outlook. This phenomenon has been universal.

1. NECESSITY OF LABOUR WELFARE WORK IN INDIA

As regards the necessity of welfare work in India, it can be easily realised if we look into the conditions of working classes in our country. They have to work for long hours under unhealthy surroundings and afterwards, have no means to remove the drudgery of their lives. Removed from the village community, and thrown into a strange and uncongenial environment, they are liable to become easy victims of drinks, gambling and other vices, which tend towards their demoralisation and ruin. Indian workers regard industrial employment as a necessary evil, from which they are eager to escape as early as possible. A contented, stable and efficient labour force, therefore, cannot be built up without an improvement in the conditions of their life and work in industrial centres. The importance of welfare work is, therefore, greater in India than in the west. There can be no doubt as regards the beneficial effect of welfare measures, such as educational facilities, sports, entertainments, etc., on the sentimental atmosphere in the factory and their contribution to the maintenance of industrial peace. When the worker feels that the employer and the State are interested in his day-to-day life and would like to make his lot happier in every possible way, his tendency to grouse and grumble will steadily disappear. Besides, welfare activities carried on in the mills would contribute in making service in the mills attractive to labour and would create a permanent settled labour force. Things like good housing, canteens, sickness and other benefits, etc., are bound to create a feeling amongst the workers that they have a stake in the industry, as much as any one else, and would greatly reduce labour turnover and absenteeism and would improve workers' efficiency. The social advantages of welfare activities are also very great. The provision of canteens, where cheap, clean and balanced food is available to workers, must improve their physique; entertainments must reduce the incidence of vices; medical, maternity and child welfare facilities must improve the health of the workers and their families and bring down the rates of general, maternal and infant mortality; and educational facilities must increase the mental efficiency and economic productivity.

Thus, the necessity of welfare work is now beyond the stage of debate and is recognised as an integral part of industrial management in all countries. The need for improving the material conditions of workers, both from the social view point and from the effect on productive efficiency, is being increasingly appreciated throughout the civilized world. Labour welfare plays a vital role in industrial economy. It is now an essential part of business organisation and management, which now a days attaches more importance to human angle. It increases the productive efficiency of workers and infuses in them a new spirit of self-realisation and consciousness. Labour welfare work postulates a real change of hearts and a change of outlook on the part of both the employers and the workers as parts of an integral whole. In India, which has embarked upon a vast programme of industrialisation under the Five-Year Plans, the need for labour welfare is all the more important because it creates a healthy atmosphere in the work place, keeps the labour force stable and contented and helps in maintaining industrial peace.[1]

2. CONCEPT AND SCOPE OF LABOUR WELFARE

'Labour welfare' is a nebulous terms which has been defined differently by different people. No definition has as yet received universal recognition. The *Oxford Dictionary* defines labour welfare as "efforts to make life worth living for workmen."[2] *The Encyclopaedia of Social Sciences* defines labour welfare as the "voluntary efforts of the employers to establish, within the existing industrial system, working and sometimes living and cultural conditions of the employees beyond what is required by law, the custom of industry and the conditions of the market."[3]

The Royal Commission on Labour (1931) understood labour welfare "As one which is necessarily elastic, differing from country to country, according to different social customs, degree of industrialisation and the level of educational development."[4]

N.M. Joshi felt that labour welfare "covers all the efforts which employers make for the benefit of their employees over and above the minimum standard of working conditions fixed by *The Factory Act* and over and above the provision of social legislation providing against accident, old age, unemployment and sickness."[5] *Moorthy* holds the "Labour welfare has two sides, negative and positive. On the one side it is associated with the counteracting of the harmful effects of large-scale industrialisation on the personal, family and social life of the worker while on the other positive side, it deals with the provision of opportunities for the worker and his family for a socially and personally good life."[6]

The Committee on Labour Welfare, set up by the Government of India in 1969, in its report defined labour welfare to "include such services, facilities and amenities as adequate canteens, rest and recreation facilities, sanitary and medical facilities, arrangements for travel to and from work and for the accommodation of workers employed at a distance from their homes and such other services, amenities and facilities including social security measures as contribute to improve the conditions under which workers are employed."

The International Labour Organisation also observed that the term is one which lends itself to various interpretations, and it has not always the some significance in different countries. Sometimes the concept is a very wide one and is more or less synonymous with conditions of work as a whole. It may include not only the minimum standard of hygiene and safety laid down in general labour legislation, but also aspects of working life as social insurance schemes, measures for protection of women and young workers, limitation of hours of works, paid vacations etc."[7]

"In other cases, the definition is much more limited, and welfare, in addition to general physical working conditions, is mainly concerned with the day-to-day problems of worker and the social relationship at the place of work."[8]

Again, "In some countries the use of welfare facilities provided are confined to the workers employed in the undertaking concerned, while in others the workers families are allowed to share in many of the benefits which are made available."[9]

It is, thus obvious from the above analysis that the scope of labour welfare has been described by writers and institutions of different shades, in different ways. However it is a dynamic concept and rigid limits cannot be laid down for scope of labour welfare for all industries and for all times.

However it, is also concluded that Labour Welfare Services should:

- enable workers to live a richer and more satisfactory life;
- contribute to the productivity of labour and efficiency of the enterprise;
- raise the standard of living of the workers by indirectly reducing the burden on their purse;

- be in tune and harmony with similar services obtaining in a neighbouring community where an enterprise is situated;
- be based on an intelligent prediction of the future needs of industrial work, and be so designed as to offer a cushion to absorb the shock of industrialisation and urbanisation on workers; and
- be administratively viable and essentially developmental in outlook.

The scope of labour welfare needs to be considered pragmatically, and has to be both dynamic and elastic. Statutory welfare measures in industry may stem from the direct concern for efficiency and productivity. But, to the extent these measures are employee-oriented, they should be considered to fall within the scope of labour welfare. Non-Statutory measures or those developed in response to the demands of technology also fall in the same category. Several extra-mural services such as company, housing and schools, recreation and community centres, sports and other cultural activities fall within the purview of labour welfare. Thus, it would be clear that we are inclined to regard all extra and intra-mural as well as statutory and non-statutory welfare measures of employers, government, and trade unions as falling within the scope of term labour welfare. Till the community can afford to have a comprehensive social security scheme, such measures can legitimately be considered as labour welfare.[10]

3. THEORIES OF LABOUR WELFARE

A theory here means or includes a statement or formulations of principles, assumptions and presumptions which provide rational explanation to labour welfare. To different men various theories seem appropriate.

I. The Policy Theory

This is based on the contention that a minimum standard of welfare is necessary for labourers. Hence the assumption is that, without compulsion, periodical supervision and fear of punishment, employers will not provide even the minimum welfare facilities for workers. Apparently, this theory assumes that man is selfish and self-centred, and always tries to achieve his own ends, even at the cost of welfare of others. The Policy Theory therefore, leads to:

1. The passing of laws relating to the provision of minimum welfare for workers.
2. Periodical supervision to ascertain that these welfare measures are being provided and implemented; and
3. Punishment of employers who evade or disobey these laws.

In this theory, the emphasis is unfortunately on form and not on the spirit of welfare which should be guiding factor. However, in a country like India, where working conditions in many places are not at all congenial and where the majority of workers are illiterate, a certain amount of coercion is essential in the interests of working population.

II. The Religious Theory

This is based on the concept that man is essentially "an animal". Even today many acts of man are related to religious sentiments and beliefs. Thus, according to this theory, any good work is considered "an investment": both the benefactor and the beneficiary are rewarded. Another aspect of this religious theory is the atonement aspect. Some people take up welfare work in spirit of atonement for their sins. Thus, the benevolent acts of welfare are treated either as an investment or an atonement.

According to this theory, man is primarily concerned with his own welfare and only secondarily, with the welfare of others. The religious basis of welfare, however, cannot be rational. It is neither universal nor continuous.

III. Philanthropic Theory

This theory is based on man's love for mankind. "In Greek, *philos* means loving *anthropes* means man". So philanthropic means *"loving mankind"*. Man is believed to have an instinctive urge by which he strives to remove the suffering of others and promote their well-being. When some employers have compassion for their fellowmen, they may undertake welfare measures for the benefit of their workers.

This theory thus depends largely on man's love for others, and therefore, cannot be universal or continuous. Irregular and occasional philanthropic acts of welfare may sometimes defeat the very purpose of welfare.

IV. Trusteeship Theory

This is also called the Paternalistic Theory of Labour Welfare according to which "the industrialist or employer holds the total industrial estate, properties, and profits accruing from them in trust." The main emphasis here is on the idea that employers should provide, out of the funds under their control, for the well-being of their workers. Mahatma Gandhi very strongly advocated this Trusteeship Theory.

Here too, labour welfare depends on the initiative of the top management. Since, it has no legal sanction, its value is related to the moral conscience of the industrialist. Also, this theory treats "workers as perpetual minors and industrialists as eternal guardians." The self-reliant growth of the trade union movement is ignored in this theory, though it may create a basis of goodwill between labour and management.

V. The Placating Theory

This theory is based on the fact that labour groups are becoming demanding and militant, and are more conscious of their rights and privileges than ever before. Their demand for higher wages and better standards cannot be ignored. According to this theory, timely and periodical acts of labour welfare can appease to workers. They are some kind of pacifiers by way of friendly gesture.

Sincerity may lack in these programmes, though discontent can be bought off in this manner. Psychologically, this theory is unsound, though it has often been acted upon to secure the workers co-operation.

VI. Public Relations Theory

This theory provides the basis for an atmosphere of goodwill between labour and management and the public. Labour welfare programmes, under this theory, work as a sort of an advertisement and help an industrialist to build up good and healthy public relations. This theory is based on the assumption that the labour welfare movement may be utilised to improve relations between management and labour.

But this kind of programme may also lack in sincerity and continuity. When such a programme loses its advertisement value, it may be neglected by the employers even though it is still useful for employees. Here welfare may tend to become a publicity stunt. Nevertheless, these programmes do improve industrial relations.

VII. The Functional Theory

This is also called the Efficiency Theory. Here welfare work is used as a means to secure, preserve and develop the efficiency and productivity of labour. It is obvious that if an employer takes good care of his workers, they will tend to come to be more efficient and will thereby step up production. This theory is reflection of the contemporary support for labour welfare. It can work well if both the parties have an identical aim in mind, that is, higher production through better welfare. And this will encourage labour's participation in welfare programmes.[11]

These theories treat labour welfarism as different people look at it. These articulate the rationale behind welfarism. As no two persons think in the same way, a philosopher, a philanthropists, a social worker, a trade unionist and the like must think of labour welfare differently. In each theory there is an aspect of truth. Consistent with the value ethos of a society one theory may be more relevant than the other. But, no one single theory articulates all the justification on reason. Taken together they articulate, rationalise and pragmatise the labour welfarism.

In India, it is said, the industrial system clings largely to the paternalistic approach. Some managements, however, obliged to achieve results through police control. Either way, workers start expecting two much from employers, as a result of which employers provide welfare measures in a somewhat half hearted manner. The trusteeship theory too, can be applied suitably in Indian conditions, though in the longer run, it is better to act on the basis of the functional theory of labour welfare, for it works more effectively by reason of ensuring an intelligent and willing participation of workers.[12]

4. PRINCIPLES OF LABOUR WELFARE

Labour welfare is dependent on certain basic principles, which must be kept in mind and properly followed to achieve a successful implementation of welfare programmes.[13]

I. Principle of Adequacy of Wages

Labour welfare measures cannot be substituted for wages. Workers have a right to adequate wages. But high wage rates along cannot create a healthy atmosphere nor bring about a sense of commitment on the part of workers. A combination of social welfare, educational welfare and economic welfare together would achieve good results.

II. Principle of Social Responsibility of Industry

Industry according to this principle, has an obligation or duty towards its employees to look after their welfare. The Constitution of India, in its Directive Principles of State Policy, also emphasises upon the aspect of labour welfare.

III. Principle of Efficiency

It plays an important role in welfare services. This is based on the relationship between welfare and efficiency, though it is difficult to measure the relationship. Whether one accepts responsibility for implementing such labour welfare measures as would increase efficiency.

IV. Principle of Re-personalisation

The development of the human personality is given here as the goal of industrial welfare, which, according to this principle, should complement the beneficial effects of the industrial system. Therefore, it is necessary to implement labour welfare services both inside and outside the factory, that is, to provide intra-mural and extra-mural labour welfare services.

V. Principle of Totality of Welfare

The principle emphasis that the concept of labour welfare must spread throughout the hierarchy of an organisation. Employees at all levels must accept this total concept of labour welfare because, without this acceptance, labour welfare programmes will never really get off the ground.

VI. Principle of Association or Democratic Value

The co-operation of the worker is the basis of this principle. Consultation with, and the agreement of, the workers in formulation and implementation of labour welfare services are very necessary for their success. Moreover workers who have a part in planning these programmes get keenly interested in their proper implementation.

VII. Principle of Timeliness

The timeliness of any service help in its success. To find out what the labour problem is and to discover what kind of help is necessary to solve the problem and when to provide this help, are all very necessary in planning labour welfare programmes. Timely action in the proper direction is essential in any kind of social work.[14]

5. LABOUR WELFARE PRACTICES IN INDIA

I. Welfare Facilities within the Precincts of the Establishment

Intra-Mural Labour Welfare Activities are those amenities which are provided within the precincts of the establishment.

(a) Sanitary and Hygiene Facilities

The maintenance of a clean, sanitary and hygienic work environment is now taken for granted as an important basic welfare amenity. This includes toilets, water for drinking and washing. Sanitary and hygienic conditions were extremely poor when *The Labour Investigation Committee, 1946* reported. The Committee observed that, "apart from making the minimum arrangement which an enterprise could get away with, service and maintenance appeared to be so poor that if they existed at all, the workers felt it impossible to make use of so the so-called facilities."

The Factories Act, 1948 requires that every factory must be kept clean and free from effuvia flowing from any drain or privy. A sufficient supply of wholesome, drinking water must be made available at suitable and convenient points; that separate latrines and urinals for male and female workers must be provided.

However, there are certain problems which should also be stated here.

In the *first place,* many employers in a large number of workshops and handicraft establishments, cannot by reason of their limited means satisfy the minimum conditions regarding sanitary and hygiene facilities. *Secondly,* workers ignorance and ingrained habits, too, are responsible for unsatisfactory conditions of toilets and washing place maintained by industrial undertakings.

It is therefore, suggested that these problems should be tackled at all levels and employers should go ahead in providing better facilities to their workers.

(b) *Washing Facilities*

It was *The Royal Commission on Labour* which noted that the provision of suitable washing facilities for all employees through desirable was deficient in many factories. The worker who lives in crowded areas has inadequate facilities for washing and bathing etc. at home. The Commission recommended that for workers engaged in dirty processes, suitable washing place and water should be made available compulsorily.

Bathing and washing facilities are now provided by every employer where *Factory Act, 1948, Coal Mines Act, 1952 and Plantation Labour Act, 1951* is applicable, irrespective of the number of workers employed therein. It is now the statutory responsibility of the employers. Every modern and bigger employer is providing this facility to the workers. But, in case of small scale enterprises and workshops, such as printing press, handloom units and cane crushers and such other enterprises, conditions are not satisfactory.

(c) *Drinking Water*

It is pointed out that most factories made some provision for drinking water, but the arrangements are neither uniform nor satisfactory. In textile mills, factories, bidi works, tanneries, printing presses, glass and sugar factories, mines and plantations, no arrangements generally existed; where they did, they were although unsatisfactory. However, it was only in cement factories that there were satisfactory arrangements for supply of drinking water.

Now, it is statutory obligation upon the employers to make satisfactory arrangements for drinking water to their works. All employers are required to make satisfactory arrangements for drinking water under *The Factories Act, 1948, Coal Mines Act, 1952, Plantation Labour Act, 1951,* irrespective of the size of establishment. At present almost all large scale industries have made satisfactory arrangements for drinking water. But, satisfactory arrangements for drinking water are not being made in small scale industries, since these units suffer from shortage of finance.

(d) First Aid Box

Maintenance of first aid box for every factory employing 150 workers is a minimum "must" which cannot be allowed to be ignored by any occupier of a factory establishment. This is a provision which is not generally taken seriously although the utility of it can hardly be minimised or considered superfluous. However, *The Labour Welfare Committee (1969)* recommended that, this provision should be enforced strictly and sufficient number of personnel be trained in all establishments in consultation and co-operation with the respective authorities and trade unions.[15]

(e) Rest Shelter Facilities

The Labour Investigation Committee pointed out that rest shelters were provided by only a small number of concerns. Where rest shelters were provided, their structure usually considered of bricks, walls and roof of corrugated iron sheets. In a number of cases the wall were Kutcha. They were put up at any place convenient to the employers. There sheds could not accommodate all or even most of the workers. Now rest shelter facility has become a statutory obligation on the part of the employers. These facilities help to reduce fatigue.

The Factories Act, 1948, requires that suitable sitting arrangements are to be made and maintained for all workers who are obliged to work standing. At present most of the large-scale industries, and modern undertakings provide pleasant comfortable rest rooms. Here, it can be concluded that the rest facilities are satisfactorly provided in large-scale industries and modern undertakings. But smaller units and the more traditional ones have not bothered much about this welfare amenity.

(f) Canteens

The Royal Commission on Labour, 1928 and *The Labour Investigation Committee, 1946* laid considerable emphasis on the provision of canteen inside the work place. *The Labour Investigation Committee* realised the importance of canteen as a welfare amenity. It said, that the workers canteen is increasingly recognised all over the world as an essential part of the industrial establishment, providing undeniable benefits from the point of view of health, efficiency and well-being.

In most of the developed countries, canteen have already become a long standing feature of the industrial life. However, in a majority of the developing countries canteens are not generally prevalent in medium size and small undertakings unless there is legislation empowering the competent to require the setting up of canteens in all undertakings employing more than a certain number of workers as in Bruma, India and Pakistan.

In India, it is a statutory obligation to provide facility of canteen where 150 or more workers are working in a factory. *The Factory Act, 1948* requires that every factory employing 150 or more workers should have a lunch room, with provision for drinking water, to enable works, to eat the meals brought by them; and where 250 or more workers are employed, there should be a canteen or canteens and a Bipartite Canteen Committee. *The Plantation Labour Act, 1951* requires that all plantations employing 50 or more workers should provide the facility of canteens to their workers. *The Mines Act, 1952* requires that all the mines where the number of workers is 50 or more should provide suitable shelters where workers may have their meals, and where 250 persons or more are working, the mines should provide canteens.

It has also been observed that the standard of canteens varies from unit to unit. The bigger undertakings and the more enlightened managements in the private and public sectors, have provided modern clean canteens with up-to-date equipments such as electric cookers. But in the smaller and medium sized undertakings, canteens are note properly organised.[16]

Malviya Committee recommended that the management/ employers should provide canteen facility even in establishments employing less than the prescribed limit for workers.

(g) Creches

It is a welfare facility which is provided for women workers. A Creche is defined as a place where babies of working mothers are taken care of, while mothers are at work.

The need for the establishments of Creche in industrial units was stressed as far back as 1931 when the *Royal Commission on Labour* recommended that the provision of Creches should be made a statutory obligation in all factories employing not less than 250 women.

The provisions of a Creche was first made in *The Factories Act of 1934*. But *The Factory Act of 1948* emphasised its necessity and made specific provision. *The Factory Act of 1948,* requires that a Creche must be maintained in all factories where more than 50 women workers are ordinarily employed. In mines *The Mines Creche Rules, 1966* requires that the owner/agent/ manager of a mine which employs minimum women should provide Creche at the mine for the children under six years of age. *The Plantation Labour Act, 1951,* provides that all plantations, where 50 or more women workers are employed should provide and maintain a suitable room for the use of children of such women who are below the age of six years.

The employers have maintained that Creches have been provided, both in letter and spirit, wherever their establishments are under obligation to do so. The workers have been contending that the position is not satisfactory as the employers portray it. However, the *Labour Welfare Committee which is popularly known as Malviya Committee observed* that "some of the establishment had very good Creches, properly manned and run, as per rules laid down under *The Factories Act*. Others were below standard in more than one respect." I thus, reveals a mixed picture.

The Committee recommended that the standards prescribed in law in respect of Creches should be strictly maintained and even if the number of children attending Creches decreases, there standards should not be allowed to go down.

II. Welfare Facilities Outside the Precincts of the Establishment

The welfare facilities provided outside for workplace are generally non-statutory in nature, and include housing, recreation, medical and transport facilities etc.

(a) Medical Facilities

The importance of industrial health and core in general has been emphasised by *The International Labour Organisation since 1919. The Royal Commission on Labour in 1931* and *The Labour Investigation Committee in 1946* also emphasised the necessity of providing basic health and medical facilities to industrial workers, since it will help to reduce the incidence of sickness and, therefore, absenteeism among them and increase productivity.

The Factory Act of 1948 provided for cleanliness disposal of wastes and effluents, dust and fume, artificial humidification, restriction regarding over-crowding, lighting, drinking water etc. It is obligatory upon the employers to maintain first aid-kit and ambulance in all factories where 500 or more workers are working. The statutory medical facilities are provided in Industries under the *Employees State Insurance Act, 1948* with subsequent amendments. This Act extends benefits to industrial workers, such as (i) Maternity benefits, (ii) Disablement benefits, (iii) Dependent benefits, (iv) Sickness benefits, (v) Medical benefits. The families of the workers are also covered to some extent under this Act. At present, in mines, elaborate arrangements have been made for medical facilities to workers employed in collieries by the *Coal Mines Labour Welfare Fund Organisation* through a net-work of hospitals and dispensaries including Ayurvedic dispensaries.

It has been observed that big undertakings-situated in out of the way locations or in accessible areas like mines and plantations or steel plants which have created new industrial townships—have provided a wide range of medical facilities. On the other hand, smaller and unregulated workshops and small scale and seasonal industries are lacking in providing these basic medical amenities and, therefore, arrangements should we made to have at least first aid and out-patient dispensary service for workers in these industries.

(b) Educational Facilities

The need for imparting necessary education to workers in India has been emphasised by the *Indian Industrial Commission (1981), The Royal Commission on Labour (1931)* and *The National Commission on Labour* (1966). The Indian Industrial Commission observed that "A factor which has tended in the past to delay the progress of Indian Industrial development had been the ignorance and conservatism of the uneducated women." *The Royal Commission of Labour* stated that "In India nearly the whole mass of Industrial Labour is illiterate, a state of affairs which is unknown in any other country of industrial importance. Modern machine industry depends in particular degree on education and the attempt to build it up with an illiterate body of workers must be difficult and perilous."

Though considerable improvement has taken place in the general standard of literary and education of working class since the observations of these Commissions, the overall position with regard to the preponderance of illiteracy amongst working population continues.

The statutory obligation of providing educational facilities for workers children exists only in plantation industry. No other industry, manufacturing or mining, is bound by law in this matter.

The Malviya Committee on Labour Welfare pointed out that the general attitude of the employers both in manufacturing and mining industries where the provision of educational facilities to workers children is not obligatory is that, it is primarily the business of the State to provide both primary and secondary educational facilities to workers children as in the case on citizens.

(c) Recreational Facilities

Recreation has an important bearing on the development

of the individual's personality as well as on his capacity to contribute to social development. A person engaging himself in recreation chooses to do so without any compulsion, but with an urge from within. More often than not, participation in recreation brings him mental and psychological satisfaction in terms of self-expression, fund and frolic, relaxation and refreshment, joy and laughter.

In India, a number of recreational facilities have been provided to industrial workers. Some are given statutorily or voluntarily by employers; and some are provided by trade unions and social welfare agencies. Provision of recreational amenities have been made obligatory on employers in plantations. In case of Coal, Mica and Iron Ore Mines recreational facilities are provided with the help of employers and Welfare Funds established in respective mines.

At present, in large establishments increasing attention has been paid to recreational activities. But many small and medium sized undertakings, however, pay very little attention to these recreational and cultural facilities, perhaps because they do not have adequate funds for the purpose. Similarly, workers in small coal mines have been neglected. And, in mines other than coal mines, the position is still worse. In general the conditions, in mines cannot be said to be satisfactory.

The National Commission on Labour pointed out that the employers complain that the workers do not avail themselves of the amenities provided to them, on other hand, the workers maintain that the scale of facilities is very inadequate.

The Malviya Committee recommended that the Central Board of Workers Education, the All India Council of Sports, Statutory Labour Welfare Boards and allied institutions should jointly form a Council under the aegis of Ministeries on Labour and Health and Family Planning and the Ministeries of Labour and to lay the standard of recreational sports activities which could faithfully provide base for keeping the workers fit, active and healthy.

(d) Transport Facilities

In all countries of the world mobility and accessibility made possible by modern transportation are amongst the key factors for attainment of economic and social progress. The provision of adequate and cheap transport facilities to workers residing at long distance is essential as such facilities not only relieve the workers from strain and anxiety but also provide opportunity for greater relaxation and recreation. Provision of transport facilities also helps in reducing the rate of absenteeism particularly when it is on account of late arrival.

The need for providing transport facilities has been accepted by all the parties *viz.*, State Governments, employers and workers organisations and public undertakings. It should however, be stated that in big cities local transport authorities have arranged special trains, but services to meet the needs of the general public along with the industrial workers but the facilities provided have not kept the place with rapidly growing needs. *The Malviya Committee* revealed the fact that the State Governments, employers and workers organisations have admitted that the existing public transport facilities are inadequate and cannot cater to the demands of individual workers employed in big industrial cities.[17]

In this context various measures have been suggested to meet the situation, such as increase in the number of buses and their frequency; setting up of special transport services; adjustment of staggering in hours of work in industrial establishment; adaptability to timings and routes of public transport services etc.

(e) Consumers' Co-operative Stores and Fair Price Shops

The importance of opening some special shops for the working class was realised during the Second World War when a large number of Consumers Stores were organised by the Government of India for distribution of controlled commodities. The importance of consumers' co-operative stores and fair shops was highlighted by *The National Co-operative Development* and *The Warehousing Board Committee of 1961;* by *The Indian Labour Conference in its 20th Session in 1962*. The Conference adopted a scheme for setting up consumers' co-operative stores in all industrial establishments, including plantations and mines, employing 300 or more workers.

The functioning of the scheme of co-operative consumers' stores and fair price shope was reviewed a year later by the Standing Committee on Industrial Truce Resolution in August,

1963. The Committee expressed its dissatisfaction with the progress of setting up co-operative consumers' stores. *The State Labour Ministers Conference and the Indian Labour Conference* both held in New Delhi in 1966 again took stock of the progress in the matter. They were dissatisfied with the implementation of the programme, particularly in case of private undertakings and plantations.

No legislation was, however, undertaken and persuasive efforts of the Central and State Governments continued to be made in the matter. As a result of these efforts considerable progress was made in establishments employing 300 or more workers in factories and mines. *The Malviya Committee on Labour Welfare (1969),* however, recommended that, the limit of 300 workers laid down under the existing scheme for opening a fair price shop/consumer co-operative store, should be progressively reduced so as to cover establishments employing 200 or more workers.

It can be concluded that welfare implies providing better work conditions, reasonable amenities such as drinking water, toilet, rest rooms and rest pauses etc. and services beyond job such as recreation, housing, education etc. In India concept of welfare can be divided into statutory welfare and non-statutory welfare. The statutory welfare amenities and non- statutory welfare amenities have not been properly and adequately provided, except in units managed by progressive employers or in the modern units where the technology of production requires maintenance of adequate welfare standards. In several cases, particularly in medium and small sized units, the standards are distinctly poor, arrangements for drinking water and first aid boxes and upkeep and maintenance of conservancy services are not satisfactory in these units.

Thus, there is need to extend the coverage of statutory welfare amenities and non-statutory welfare amenities, but should be done only after proper administrative arrangements can be made to ensure implementation.

Notes and References

1. R.C. Saxena, Labour Problem and Social Welfare, 1981, p. 311.
2. The Concise Oxford Dictionary, Cited by L.B. Yadav, Readings in Social and Labour Welfare, Ist edition, 2000, Vol. 3.

3. Encyclopaedia of Social Sciences, Vol. XV, 1935, p. 395.
4. Government of India, Report of the Royal Commission on Labour in India, Calcutta, Central Publications Branch, 1931, p. 261.
5. N.M. Joshi, Trade Union Movement in India, Bombay, 1927, p. 26.
6. M.V. Moorthy, Principles of Labour Welfare, Visakhapatnam, Gupta Brothers, 1968, p. 10.
7. I.L.O. Report II-Provision of facilities for the promotion of Workers Welfare, Asian Regional Conference—Nuwara Eliya Ceylon, p. 3.
8. *Ibid.*, p. 3.
9. *Ibid.*, p. 3.
10. L.B. Yadav; Readings in Social and Labour Welfare, Ist edition, 2000, Vol. 3, p. 12.
11. B.P. Tyagi, Labour Economics and Social Welfare, 9th edition, 2004, pp. 614-15.
12. L.B. Yadav, Readings in Social and Labour Welfare, Ist edition, 2000, Vol. 3, pp. 291-92.
13. Saraswathi Sankaran—Labour Welfare, Page 28, Cited by B.P. Tyagi, Labour Economics and Social Welfare, 9th edition, 2004, p. 615.
14. B.P. Tyagi, Labour Economics and Social Welfare, 9th edition, 2004, p. 617.
15. Report of the Committee on Labour Welfare, 1969, p. 29.
16. Government of Bombay: Annual Administration Report of the Factories Act, 1948, for 1957, p. 14.
17. Malviya Committee Report on Labour Welfare, p. 69.

Agencies for Labour Welfare Work

There are several agencies through which various labour welfare measures are undertaken in the interest of labour welfare measures are undertaken by Central and State Govérnments. Labour legislation has been enacted by Central and State Governments which has laid down the minimum standards of employment and working conditions. Besides, Central and State Governments, employers, workers trade unions and social organisation also work as agencies for providing facilities to the workers. Generally Labour Welfare Activities are undertaken by the following agencies:

1. WELFARE WORK BY CENTRAL GOVERNMENT

Labour Welfare Policies and Five-Year Plans

In 1947 *The International Labour Organisation* laid down the framework of labour welfare and also spelt out the services and amenities which should be included in this framework. These services related to the provision of canteens, rest and recreation facilities, sanitary and medical facilities, arrangements for travel to and from works and such other amenities add facilities, as may contribute to improve the conditions under which the workers are employed. This can be regarded as the Directive Principles for Labour Welfare Works in India.[1]

With a clear guidance of what should normally be provided under welfare amenities to workers, from this highest organisation of labour in the world, the framers of Indian Constitution paid due attention to the amelioration of the working class of the country. The Indian Constitution has made a specific mention of the duties that the State owes to the labour, to their economic upliftment and social re-generation.[2]

However, even before the adoption and promulgation of the Constitution, the base of the labour welfare amenities had been laid down. *The Factories Act, 1948* provided for certain essential welfare services. For the provision of medical and health facilities to workers outside the work place, a comprehensive legislation in the shape of the *Employees State Insurance Act was brought into being in 1948.* It provides benefit to workers in the case of sickness, maternity and employment injury, and also make provision for certain other related matters.

The Central Government policy in the field of law has been to bring matters connected with workers welfare more and more within the purview of legislation setting appropriate standards. *The Factories Act, 1948, The Plantation Labour Act, 1951* and *The Mines Act, 1952,* are basic enactments which contain elaborate provisions for safeguarding the health and safety of workers inside the workplace and for providing for their welfare. They lay down minimum standards for ensuring welfare of workers. The employers are, however, free to improve upon these minimum standards. Penal provisions in these Acts can be taken recourse to by the competent authority in the event of contravention of lapses on the part of employers. The Government of India also set up Labour Welfare Funds to provide welfare amenities for the workers employed in coal, mica, iron ore, mangnese ore, limestone and dolomite mines and in the Beedi and Cinema industries. Separate Welfare Funds have also been formed for specified services like Posts and Telegraphs, Ports, Dockyards, etc. The welfare measures financed out of the funds relate to provision of medical, housing, drinking water etc. While most of the activities are administrated directly by the Welfare Organisation under the

Ministry of Labour, Loans and Subsidies are also provided to the State Governments. Local authorities and to the employers for implementation of approved prototype schemes.[3]

The provision of social security in the form of Employees' State Insurance Scheme, provident fund, gratuity and pension under various laws and industrial housing schemes are some of the other prominent measures undertaken by the Central Government to promote welfare of the working class.[4]

The labour policy set out in the Five-Year Plans since independence was based on the belief that the basic needs of workers for food, clothing and shelter must be satisfied. *The First Plan* (Part-III, Chapter XXXIV) recommended many measures like the granting of occupancy rights for house-sites, support for the Bhoodan movement, labour cooperatives, financial assistance minimum wages, etc. for the welfare of agricultural workers.[5]

The Second Five-Year Plan (Chapter XXVII) continued the policy laid down in the First Plan with modifications that became necessary with the adoption of the goal of socialist pattern of society. There were new proposals for development programmes under labour and labour welfare. The Plan policies recommended what flowed from the ideal of welfare State. It made provision for industrial housing. The *Third Five Year Plan* made no specific reference to labour welfare, but stressed that for improving work efficiency, welfare within the establishment should be ensured. As a part of the reoriented policy, cooperative activity was identified as a labour welfare measures. *The Draft Fourth Five-Year Plan* made a significant allotment of Rs. 145 crores for schemes for training and other programmes oriented to the welfare of workers. The *draft Fifth Five Year Plan* made a provision of Rs. 57 crores for the training of craftsmen, employment service and labour welfare.[6]

The thrust of the programmes in the *Sixth Plan* (Chapter XXIV) was on the effective implementation of different legislative enactments regarding labour and special programmes for agricultural labour, artisans, handloom weavers, fishermen, leather workers and other organised workers in the rural and urban areas. The Plan emphasised vocational rehabilitation of the physically handicapped, apprenticeship and training schemes, organisation of rural workers, and problems of bonded labour, child labour, women labour, contract labour, construction labour, inter-state migrant labour, migrant shepherds, and dairy cattle owners.

The thrust of *The Seventh Plan* (Chapter V) was the improvement of capacity utilisation, efficiency and productivity. An important aspect of labour policy outlined in the Seventh Plan relate to the formulation of an appropriate wage policy and provisions for the welfare and working and living conditions of unorganised labour not only in the rural sector but also in urban areas. *The Eighth Plan* (Chapter VII) said that improvement in the quality of labour, productivity, skills and working conditions and provision of welfare and social security measures especially of those working in the unorganised sector, were crucial elements in the strategy for quantitative and qualitative enhancement of the status of labour. The Plan also laid emphasis on the enforcement of labour laws especially law relating to unorganised labour and women and child labour.[7]

However, it has to be admitted that the Five-Year Plans did not formulate an integrated and comprehensive scheme of social security for unorganised labour.[8]

2. WELFARE WORK BY STATE GOVERNMENTS

In nearly all the States and Union Territories Welfare Centres has been established to promote welfare activities for the workers and in a number of States, welfare funds have been constituted under the Acts. In these centres, facilities are provided for games, recreation library, etc.

In Andhra Pradesh, 12 Labour Welfare Centres was functioning in 1980-81 at different places for the benefit of industrial workers and their dependents and provide recreational, educational and cultural facilities. Each centre had six sections, viz., Adult education, Audio visual, Games Crafts, Nursery School and Health.

Besides, a statutory fund was created for financing welfare measures for plantation workers in Assam. *This fund was created under the Assam Plantation Employees Welfare Fund Act, 1959.* This fund is built up from the fines realised from the employees, grants from the Central/State Governments and the Tea Board, unclaimed wages and donation. The money of the Fund is utilised for activities such as adult education and literacy drives, maintaining community and social education centres, organising games and sports, excursions, tours, running holiday homes, providing training in subsidiary occupations and home industries for women and employed persons.

In Himachal Pradesh, the Labour Welfare Centre at Palampur continues to provide usual welfare facilities including in training in sewing and embroidery to women workers of plantations. In Jammu and Kashmir, there are five Labour Welfare Centres functioning within the State and five outside the State for workers migrating from the valley to the plains. These centres provides facilities for recreation, sports, newspapers, etc., as also free medical aid to the workers.

In Gujarat, Maharashtra, Mysore and Punjab, Labour Welfare Centres are administered by Welfare Boards. *The Boards of Gujarat, and Maharashtra are created under the Bombay Labour Welfare Fund Act, 1953,* and that of Mysore under the *Mysore Labour Welfare Fund Act, 1965* and that of Punjab under the *Punjab Labour Welfare Fund Act, 1965.*

Such funds are created almost in every State and welfare activities are financed from these funds. Generally, State Governments run welfare and provide following welfare facilities through them.

Recreational facilities like indoor and outdoor games, cultural activities, sports, children sports, adult educational, classes schooling of children upto nursery classes, library and reading rooms, vocational training, cultural programmes, training in tailoring and sewing, knitting, lacemaking leather and other handicrafts, medical aid, maternity and child welfare facilities. These services are provided at various labour welfare centres in accordance with the needs of industrial workers. Each centre undertakes some of these services in the light of its own finances and convenience.

Critical Estimate of Government Welfare Measures

Thus, the Governments at the Centre and in the various States have taken an active part in the labour welfare activities. However, much remains to be desired. The number of welfare centres in every State is too small, in relation to the vast size of country, industrial progress and the number of workers. More activities are also desired in the field of education and in child and maternity welfare centres. Greater attention should also be paid to the education of workers children, most of whom loiter about and indulge in bad habits at present. Medical facilities can be left to the Employees' State Insurance Corporation and Welfare Centres can expand other activities. One great defect in running these welfare centres is that the workers have little share in their management and this is one of the important causes that these centres have not achieved very great popularity and success. The labour welfare centres must have a committee of the workers to help and advise the organisers. This would ensure the active co-operation of the workers; and there would be a greater incentive to take the full advantage of the various welfare measures provided at these centres. The importance and utility of such welfare centres are undoubtedly very great, because, in a country where the workers are still unable to look after their own interest, it is the duty of the Government to provide some welfare activities and also undertake legislation to force the employers to undertake such activities.[9]

3. WELFARE WORK BY MUNICIPALITIES

There are certain municipalities which have also made provisions for the welfare of the workers. The Bombay Municipal Corporation has set up a Special Welfare Department through which it organises 15 welfare centres. These welfare centres are mostly located in the chawls of Mill workers, they assist in formation of co-operative societies and provide educational facilities, a nursery school, indoor and outdoor games, film shows, and has organised maternity facilities as well.[10]

The Madras Municipal Corporation has set-up centres for adult education through night schools, a crèche and a canteen in the corporation's workshop. The creche, under the care of a nurse and two attendants, provides workers children with cradles and toys, playground and a bathroom. A nursery school is conducted where poor children get free mid-day meals in addition to milk. Co-operative Credit Societies are also run by the Madras Municipal Corporation.

The Municipal Corporation of Calcutta has also provided somewhat similar facilities to the workers. The municipalities of Ajmer, Delhi and Kanpur have also made provisions of welfare facilities of the workers. All municipalities and corporations provide provident fund benefits. Many have made provision for retirement of gratuities as well.[11]

4. WELFARE WORK BY VOLUNTARY ORGANISATIONS

There are voluntary social service organisations which have taken interest in providing labour amenities to the workers.

The Bombay Social Service League, started by the Servants of Indian Society, conducted several activities, like promotion of education through night schools, libraries, recreation and sports. It has also secured compensation for accidents to workers, propagated the co-operative movements, promoted public health and the boy scouts movement etc.

The *Poona and Bombay Seva Sadan Societies* have taken keen interest in providing educational, medical and social services to the women and children. They have also trained social workers for this purpose.

In Bengal Women's Institute has established Mahila Samities, which visit various villages and carry on educational and public health work.

Besides, the Y.M.C.A., the Bombay Presidency Women's Council, the Maternity and Infant Welfare Association, the Depressed classes Mission Society are some of the voluntary social services agencies which have taken interest in the welfare work for industrial workers.

The voluntary social service agencies can play a more significant role in the better administration and utilisation of welfare services made available by the Government. The proper operation of statutory provisions relating to welfare can only be ensured by a strong public opinion, which in turn can be created by sustained efforts of voluntary organisations. These organisations have also played a very significant role in the industrial countries.[12]

5. WELFARE WORK BY EMPLOYERS

In the context of employers activities in the sphere of welfare, Dr. B.R. Seth observed that "The vast majority of industrialist in India still regard welfare work as a barren liability rather than a wise investment."

It may be inferred from it that most employers were indifferent towards the welfare works for their employees in the beginning of 20th century. However, there were very few employers who took the initiative in the welfare measures for the betterment of their workers. In 1915, the Calico Mills in Ahmedabad started medical services for their workers by appointing a doctor and nurse.

In 1918, in Bombay, the Tatas started a medical unit in one of their mills, which has not become the industrial health department. In 1920, in Delhi, Lala Shri Ram of Delhi Cloth Mills started housing for workers and a few other activities.

In these years, Birla Mills in Delhi, British India Corporation in Kanpur, the Empress Mills in Nagpur, the Binny Mills in Madras and Tata Steel Company in Jamshedpur had initiated Labour Welfare Programmes which were mentioned even in the Report of Royal Commission on Labour in India in 1931.[13]

The various studies conducted in this field indicate that there has been growing realisation on the part of the utility of welfare work. Welfare work, at present, is being brought more and more under the scope of legislation rather than being left to the good sense of the employers. Already, canteens, crèches, rest shelters, pit-head baths in mines, etc., have been made statutory obligations. Central and State Governments are also actively entering the field of labour welfare by providing welfare centres in industrial areas. Even so, there is still scope for individual employers, or their associations, for providing amenities and services for workers' welfare. Many enlightened employers, on their own initiative, have been doing their bit in the direction of workers' welfare, in different industries, which are mentioned below:

In Jute Mill Industry, the only employers' organisation, which has undertaken direct responsibility for organising welfare work for its member units, is the Indian Jute Mills

Association. It organised labour-welfare centres at different places, which carry out the usual welfare programmes. Besides, individual Jute mills also carry on welfare work for the workers, and have provided Labour Officers although in some they are designated as Personnel or Welfare Officers. Thirty two welfare Centres in West Bengal and one in U.P. are run by individual Jute mills.[14]

Woolen Textile Mills have varying standard of welfare activities, i.e. the standard of welfare work varies from unit to unit. The prominent mills which are providing welfare activities on extensive scales are the Dhariwal Woolen Mills, the Kanpur Woollen, Raymond Woollen Mills, and the Mahalakshmi Woollen Mills, Bombay, Lal Imli Woollen Mills. A special mention may be made of the welfare activities of the Lal Imli Woollen Mills, Kanpur. This concern has got a separate welfare section to look after labour welfare. Its main welfare activities are: provision of free education upto upper primary standard; recreational facilities; reading room and library; canteen etc. The social and religious functions on a collective basis are of great importance in the industrial establishments. A Community Hall is also maintained by the management of this undertaking. There are also two schools for boys and girls of the factory workers.

Most of the units in *The Cement Industry* maintain well-equipped hospitals manned by qualified medical officers where the workers and their families are given free medical treatment. Most units have also canteens which supply tea and snacks at cheap rates and almost all have clubs with provisions for indoor and outdoor games and reading rooms. The buildings and equipment for the schools are provided by the management and education is free. Most of the units employing women have provided creches.[15]

In Sugar Industry the standard of welfare work varies form unit to unit. A majority of the units have provided medical facilities to their workers. In some cases hospitals are also maintained. Canteens have been started by some of them while most of the units provided educational facilities. Some of them have got their own schools, while others give financial assistance to the schools attended by the workers' children.

Almost all units provide recreational facilities like sports, libraries, reading room and radio sets for the workers.

Critical Estimate of Welfare Work by Employers

It has been noticed that the voluntary welfare work undertaken by employers, in many cases, has been done grudgingly and in a patronising spirit. There has been very little real spirit of service, and things have usually come from them in an ill-grace. Many workers look on the welfare work undertaken by the employers with suspicion. The fear has been expressed that unless the workers are on their guard, "welfare" may be substituted in effect for part of the wages. Such vindictive use of welfare activities must necessarily have unfortunate consequences in the long run.

The Labour Investigation Committee also pointed out that there was a majority of the employers who took a most different and non-chalant attitude towards welfare work. Hence, the Committee remarked: "It is apparent that unless the precise responsibilities of employers in regard to welfare work are defined by law such employers are not likely to fall in line with their more enlightened and farsighted confrers." However, it has also to be noted that some excellent work has been done by some of the enlightened employers and therefore, whether this suspicion is warranted or not depends on particular employers and circumstances. It may only be pointed out that, in the administration of welfare work, employers should not have the sole powers but the workers may also be adequately represented.[16]

6. WELFARE WORK BY WORKERS' ORGANISATIONS

A few workers organisations are also engaged in welfare work for the industrial employees. The most important among them are the Textile Labour Association Ahmedabad and the Steel Employees Welfare Association (SEWA) of Bhilai Steel Plant. SEWA is implementing a scheme for social security of its members by providing financial assistance to the families of deceased members and to the members themselves in case of medical unfitness, prolonged sickness, retirement, resignation, termination, etc. All employees of the Bhilai Steel Plant are *ipso facto* members of SEWA unless he/she desired to remain out of it and gave it in writing.

The contribution of the Textile Labour Association, Ahmedabad in organising labour welfare activities has been very impressive. It actively participates in intra-mural as well as extra-mural welfare activities. The TLA spends a fair share of its income on welfare facilities. According to *The Report of Welfare Committee, 1969,* which is popularly known as *Malviya Committee,* it spends 60 per cent to 80 per cent of its income on welfare activities. It has undertaken the problem of slum areas with the help of over 250 volunteers, who were trained for this work, which covers the problem of community life as well.[17]

With Janta Insurance Policies and other programmes to relieve workers from poverty and unemployment, the TLA encouraged small saving among the workers.

It has started a Workers Cooperative Bank to which are attached consumer societies, many credit societies and also a number of workers housing cooperative societies.

Besides, the Textile Labour Association runs a number of reading rooms and libraries in working class localities. It also runs typewriting classes in working class localities. In the same way, women training courses in sewing, embroidery, etc., were being conducted.

It provides legal help to worker-members when they are involved in industrial disputes, and trains them in trade unionism and citizenship.

The Malviya Committee Report on Welfare said that the following figures speak the creditability of the TLA's welfare activities. The Association maintained 22 centres for training women in handicrafts; two study homes and one hostel for girls; five nursery schools; 16 welfare centres for the children; 39 consumers cooperative stores; 59 cooperative credit societies; 193 housing societies among the working classes, under the Cooperative Housing Scheme, the workers had constructed 1089 houses during the year 1970-71.[18]

The Mazdoor Sabha of Kanpur has also done some work in the field of labour welfare. It has maintained a reading room, a library and also a dispensary for the workers. It organises social and cultural gatherings.

The Indian Federation of Labour has organised nearly 48 labour welfare centres which undertake different types of welfare activities. It organises indoor and outdoor games, medical educational and recreational facilities through labour welfare centres.

Now, other workers organisations are also taking interest in this aspect of workers life outside the factory. The TLA itself has expanded its work with a view to encourage the spirit of self-help and co-operation among workers families.

The National Commission on Labour pointed out that similar works are also done in plantations. The Commission also pointed out that educational/cultural programmes are increasingly becoming a part of the activities of well organised unions.[19]

Therefore, it can be concluded that welfare work should be considered a joint responsibility of the employers, the State and the trade unions. They should all work in harmony to raise the standard of living of the workers. The problem of workers' welfare is of such a great magnitude that no single agency alone can tackle it successfully. On the whole, however, the State should take the responsibility of seeing that the lot of workers is improved, and happily, in most of the civilized countries of the world, the Governments have become aware of the importance of welfare work and big schemes of labour welfare and social security have been adopted by them. In India, a beginning has been made in this direction but still there is a great scope for improving and extending the welfare activities for the working classes in the country.

Notes and References

1. B.P. Tyagi, Labour Economics and Social Welfare, 9th edition, 2004, p. 645.
2. *Ibid.*
3. *Ibid.*, p. 646.
4. *Ibid.*, p. 646.
5. Report of the Second National Commission on Labour, 2002, Vol. I, (Part I), p. 753.
6. *Ibid.*
7. Report of the Second National Commission on Labour, 2002, Vol. I, (Part I), p. 754.

8. *Ibid.*
9. R.C. Saxena, Labour Problem and Social Welfare, 1981, pp. 322-23.
10. B.P. Tyagi, Labour Economics and Social Welfare, 9th edition, 2004, pp. 673-74.
11. *Ibid.*, p. 674.
12. *Ibid.*, p. 675.
13. Seth, B.R., Labour Welfare Work—U.P. Labour Bulletin, June 1942, Cited by B.P. Tyagi, Labour Economics and Social Welfare, 9th edition, 2004, p. 657.
14. R.C. Saxena, Labour Problem and Social Welfare, 1981, p. 326.
15. B.P. Tyagi, Labour Economics and Social Welfare, 9th edition, 2004, p. 662.
16. R.C. Saxena, Labour Problem and Social Welfare, 1981, pp. 335-36.
17. B.P. Tyagi, Labour Economics and Social Welfare, 9th edition, 2004, p. 671.
18. *Ibid.*, p. 673.
19. *Ibid.*

5

Social Security and its Scope

Social security has assumed considerable importance in the recent years. It is one of the basic needs in a welfare State like India. It is based on the ideal of human dignity and social justice. The underlying idea behind social security measure is that a citizen who has contributed or is likely to contribute to his country's welfare should be given protection against certain hazards. The importance of social security in developmental plans, particularly in the context of present employee and employer relations need not be exaggerated. It is a novel concept in the field of business management and industrial administration. In rudimentary form, however social security was not unknown in ancient India. Today the worker gets all his facilities as of right, decades ago he got then *en gratis*. It is true for all countries although there is no denying that social security, today embraces a wider field than even before. In addition to labour welfare and economic protection of workers it covers also socio-economic progress and development of the weaker classes.[1]

1. EVOLUTION OF SOCIAL SECURITY

At all times and in every society, at every stage of development, there have been sick people requiring medical aid and care, handicapped and old people unable to work for a living.[2] Quite apart from this there are people who are unemployed and are unable to make both ends meet. According to *Sir William Beverage*, "there are five giants on the road of reconstruction."[3] These are want, disease, ignorance, squalor and idleness.[4] The fear created by these giants have crossed the limit where individuals could not have controlled them individually or in small groups.

In the early days when human needs were limited and livelihood was based primarily on agriculture, joint families, craft guilds, churches, charitable, philanthropic and other religious institutions provided these securities. In some countries poor houses were also established. However the system based on voluntary charity proved to be inadequate and unsatisfactory later on. In some countries these were supplemented with mutual benefit schemes and State aids.

Before the advent of the modern Industrial Revolution in the 18th century, all over the world, industry used to be just a domestic enterprise. In the early phase of the Industrial Revolution, the profit motive of the investors and share-holders was dominent and, as such, the worker developed as a commodity to be hired and fired in the interest of more and more of profits for capitalist investors. The dominant profit motive thriving under the non-intervention of the State and seeking to revolutionise production with its competitive aims and methods, exploited and debased on increasing number of workers who were drawn to it as wage-earners. The theory of a *"exploitation of man by man is the bitter fruit of profit motive"* dominant those days.

Under *Laissez Fair* economy, the workers suffered owing to the long hours of work, having to work in most unhealthy surroundings, exposure to accidents and, above all, low wages which did not provide even bare subsistence. With the deepening of the Industrial Revolution, institutions like joint family system, family guilds, charitable societies and organisation became inadequate.

Today when the world is passing through an industrial era and life is becoming more and more individualistic yet complex and complicated because of industrial and scientific advancement, the risk of life have increased manifold.

The advent of Industrial Revolution brought within its train great and far-reaching institutional and technological changes. It has brought changes of fundamental nature in the social culture milieu. Although modern industrialism has opened new vistas of material advancement, it has at the same time made the industrial working class more vulnerable to social contingencies. Therefore, a clamour for higher wages, better working conditions, comprehensive protection through social security measures and workers participation in management will continue till eternity under the new schemes of things.

With the growth of the modern factory system of production has also grown a demand for institutionalising contingency protection. In 1878, *Otto Von Bismark* of Prusia enacted the *Employers' Liability Act.* The Act made the employer "responsible in case of all injuries not due to the workman's own fault, for loss of wages, medical expenses, and in case of death, compensation to dependents and funeral expenses."[5] A contributory sickness benefit scheme was also introduced in 1883 by *Bismark.*

In the early twentieth century, many countries had enacted social assistance measures particularly for old age assistance. It is said, however, that the schemes of social assistance and social insurance grew like patchworks and no attempt was consciously made for providing comprehensive protection. Conscious planning in this field may be said to have begun in the year 1919 when the *International Labour Organisation* was set-up at Geneva. The ILO began to work as a specialised agency for protecting the interests of the workers by securing the collaboration and co-operation of the Governments, employers and the workers of the member countries. It has helped in the standardisation of the social security practice all over the world. The ILO also issued a survey into the social security measures of the world and published it in 1942 under the title of *"Approaches to Social Security"*. It issued another publication: *Social Security: Principles and Problems, Arising out of War* in 1944 which recommended a comprehensive scheme of social security and medical care as a measure of post war construction. This was the first conscious effort by the ILO to consolidate the individual measures of relief into a full grown social security scheme providing protection from womb to tomb.[6]

The Social Reform Act, 1933 of the Social Democratic Government in Denmark codified, simplified and extended previous social insurance and assistance legislation. *The Social Security Act, 1935,* passed by the Roosevelt administration in the U.S.A. was the first official use of the term *"social security"*, though the provisions of the Act were limited. The term 'social security' originated in United States and spread throughout the world. The *Labour Government's Social Security Act, 1938 in New Zealand* provided the most comprehensive interpretation of social security at that time.[7]

The Publication of *Beveridge Report on Social Insurance and Allied Services in 1942,* laid the foundation of the present social security system of Great Britain which provides protection to the entire population against all social and biological contingencies. *The Marsh Report on Social Security for Canada, 1943* and the *Wagner-Murray-Dingell Bill* introduced in United States Congress in June 1943 summed up the thinking of the experts at that time on the feasibility and desirability of comprehensive schemes of social security. In the post war years, a number of countries have attempted comprehensive schemes with good success.[8]

This trend towards comprehensive social security planning found expression in two International events. The 26th Session of the International Labour Conference in Philadelphia in 1994 adopted two recommendations dealing with social security. Income security and Medical care. The Declaration of Philadelphia included the extension of social security measures to provide a basic income to all in need of such protection and comprehensive medical care. The second event was the change in 1947 of the name of the International Social Insurance Conference to the International Social Security Association.[9]

In India the social security measures were taken under the provisions of various social security enactments. The British rulers generally modelled Indian labour laws on the British Legislation such as *Factories Act, 1948, The Workmen's*

Compensation Act, 1923 and The Trade Union Act, 1926. In the meanwhile, the Indian Labour Movement become linked with the International Labour Movement. In 1929, the Royal Commission on Labour, presided over by *J.H. Whittey,* was appointed. Its reports and recommendations became the foundation of labour legislation in India till the advent of congress Ministery. However, it was mainly after the independence that India could take up the problem of social security at par with all advanced countries of the world in a planned and coordinated manner.

The National Commission on Labour, 2002 accepts the need of social security as a fundamental human right. *The National Commission on Labour, 2002* is of the view that no single approach to provide social security, will be adequate. The problem has to be addressed by multi pronged approach that would be relevant in the Indian context.[10]

2. THE MEANING OF SOCIAL SECURITY

Social security is a dynamic concept. Being a dynamic subject no rigid limit can be laid down for all time to come. It varies from time to time and country to country. Social security may provide for the welfare of persons who become incapable of working by reason of old age, sickness and invalidity and are unable to earn anything for their livelihood.

The word, first used by *Bismark* in eighteen eightees in Germany, could get its official recognition and was authoritatively used in the U.S.A. only in 1935 for the first time. According to an *American Committee of Experts,* social security is, "security for employment, security in the availability of employment, security of reasonable standard of working conditions, security of some income while unemployed, security of retirement income, of recreation of self improvement of medical and ill health, or death."

It we examine this definition it seems clear that basically the concept of social security is co-terminus with the concept of progress.

The first systematic attempt to define social security was made by *International Labour Organisation* which defines social security as "the security that society furnishes through appropriate organisations against certain risk to which its members are exposed."[11] This definition indicates that social security is a provision made by the society. It is social because it represents the culmination of collective efforts, secondly, the provision is organised one. It is not haphazard or dependent upon the resources and the will of these agencies responsible for its dispensation. It is a provision against certain risks only. However it may be noted that the above definition is vague and indeterminate since it does not specify what kind of security is envisaged under the scheme and against what kind of risks.[12]

Lord Beveridge in his report on social insurance and Allied Services used the term social security meaning thereby the security of an income to take the place of earning when they are interrupted by unemployment, sickness or accident, to provide for retirement through age, to provide against loss of support by the death of another person and to meet exceptional expenditures, such as those compared with birth and death. The definition logically speaking, is too wide and comprehensive both since it does not specify the protection to be provided for labour community in modern industrial structure.

Cassidy defines social security as a scheme that connotes particularly measures of income maintenance or income security.[13] However, this definition is too narrow and vague. Broadly speaking the term social security is usually employed to indicate 'specific government programmes designed primarily to prevent want by assuring to families the basic means of subsistence.[14] This also represent narrow outlook towards social security measures.

International Labour Organisation has redefined the term social security in better words as only such schemes as provide the citizens with bebefit designed to prevent or cure disease, to support him when unable to earn and restore him to gainful activity. This definition seem to be appropriate to a greater extent. However, the definition has laid an emphasis on the working devices which are simply the means to achieve the objective of social security. It does not indicate clearly distinction between the measures of social security and the idea of social security itself.

Social security, according to *New Zealand Royal Commission*, should ensure that everyone is able to enjoy a standard of living like that of the rest of the community, and thus is able to feel a sense of participation in and belonging to the community.

In India, the *National Commission on Labour* has endorsed the ILO definition of social security and observes:

Social security envisages that the members of a community shall be protected by collective action against social risks causing undue hardship and privation to individuals whose prime resources can seldom be adequate to meet them.[15]

According to present day conditions, social security covers up programmes of protecting the old and invalid. In the States where the scheme had its birth in modern form, the programme includes quite a number of schemes, e.g. survivor's insurance, health and maternity insurance, workmen's compensation, unemployment insurance and family allowances. It does not mean that these schemes fell outside the scope of governmental activities of welfare earlier. They were certainly that but not in a coordinated pattern as in modern times.[16]

It may be submitted that concept of social security should be viewed in the context of socio-economic conditions which are determined by the political philosophy and policy of the State. In this context more appropriate definition may be attempted for our purposes, social security means and includes schemes and measures adopted by the State to furnish safety, relief and protection against sickness, maternity, disablement medical, dependents' funeral and employment insecurities and risks and various safeguards pertaining to health, safety, welfare and working hours in industrial establishments.

3. CONSTITUENTS OF SOCIAL SECURITY

The constituents of social security may be classified into following two categories:

I. Traditional Constituents of Social Security

The concept of social security is the product of 1930s. The social security is referred to set of measures designed to provide medical care and income security to members of the society entitled to. In actual practice, there are the following two constituents of social security *viz.* (a) Social Insurance, (b) Social Assistance.

Social assistance schemes can be adopted only when the entire population is entitled to benefits. Where benefits are conferred on a selected class of people, it would be inequitable to finance the scheme out of general revenues and so a social insurance approach is preferable.

(a) Social Insurance

The ILO defines 'social insurance' as a scheme that provides benefits for persons of small earnings granted as of right in amounts which combine the contributive effort of the insured with subsidies from the employer and the State. Thus social insurance protects persons of small earnings. Historically, it provided protection to industrial workers in the first instance. Social insurance is a *Social* because it involves the collective efforts of the beneficiaries, their employers, if any, and the State. It is *insurance* because the beneficiary has to pay contributions before he is entitled to reveive benefits. Thus, the benefits are not paid *gratis,* they are systematically financed. Since the scheme is subsidised, a device is evolved to exclude the cases which do not deserve any subsidy from the State. Hence, almost all scheme of social insurance set a limit of income beyond which protection is not available.

In addition to this social insurance is *a compulsory measure.* The persons falling within the defined limits of the insured population cannot refused to get insured. This is done because if the scheme is made optional, the really poor would fall from the mesh as they will be the least willing to pay the contributions. Social insurance schemes often provide that those earning below a specified limit will be exempt from any contributions; but the subsidy from the employers and the State will continue to be paid. This is done in order to avoid undue hardship to the very low paid persons that they may otherwise face if the payment of contributions by them is made compulsory.[17]

To sum up, it may be observed that social insurance is compulsory in nature based on contributory principle to provide protection in specified contingencies on fulfilling specified qualifying conditions laid down under the provisions of social welfare legislations.

(b) Social Assistance

Social assistance is a device organised by the State by providing cash assistance and medical relief, to such members of the society as cannot get them from their own resources. Appropriate allowances in cash or partly in cash and partly in kind should be provided for all persons who are in want and do not require internment for corrective care.[18]

Social assistance programmes provide benefits sufficient to meet the minimum needs of persons of small means. The special characteristic of these measure is that they are financed wholly from the general revenues of the State. Benefits under the scheme of social assistance are given as a legal right to them, provided they fulfill certain conditions. The first risk to be covered was that of old age, but gradually non-contributory benefits were introduced for invalids, survivors and unemployed persons as well. *Today social assistance programmes cover programme like unemployment assistance, old age assistance and national assistance.*

The ILO defines social assistance scheme as one that provides benefits to persons of small means granted as of right in amounts sufficient to meet a minimum standard of need and financed from taxation.[19] Thus it is a scheme of institutional charity.

The Social assistance underlines the idea that the care of people could not be left to voluntary charity and should be placed on a compulsory and statutory basis. It may be argued that social assistance presumes that there is a class of people best suited to give charity and another which cannot live without charitable assistance. This is a negation of equality and social justice. The relation of workers with his employer is contractual and before law they are equal partners. This equally should be reflected in non legal institutions as well.

II. Modern Constituents of Social Security

With the completion of the Industrial Revolution the traditional institution of social security become inadequate on account of number of factors. Such as:

1. The worker's dependence on money wage became complete because of the alienation from agriculture.

2. The worker who still retained a like with the village had to fight on two fronts because of the divided and scattered family in the village and the town. It resulted into the deterioration in agriculture. But on the whole the tendency was towards the emergence of a permanent industrial working class.
3. In view of this and growth of Labour laws, child labour as a source of additional income ceased to be a useful institution for the industrial workers.
4. With the growth of industries under capitalism chronic unemployment with periodical accentuation came to stay as a feature of the economy.
5. With increased intensification of labour and/or the depletion of plants and inadequate working conditions, increasing number of industrial hazards and accidents came to be regarded as a common and almost unavoidable risk for industrial workers.[20]

On account of above factors the traditional system of social security failed to provide security measures. The concept of social welfare State came into being in modern world and thus States were assigned various functions such as education, health, labour etc. besides their essential functions. Consequently various labour welfare schemes came into operation in almost all countries of the world. As a matter of fact the concept of social security is based on ideals of human dignity and social justice. The underlying idea behind social security measures is that a citizen who has contributed or is likely to contribute to his country's welfare should be given protection against certain hazards.[21]

4. SCOPE OF SOCIAL SECURITY

A comprehensive scheme of social security covers the contingencies of sickness, maternity, occupational risks, invalidity, old age, unemployment and medical care apart from other provisions made under social assistance measures.

(a) Sickness

In the chronological order of contingency coverage,

sickness benefit schemes were started quite early. According to ILO, sickness is that contingency in which abstention from work is necessitated "on medical grounds by an acute condition due to disease or injury requiring medical treatment or supervision."[22] The test of sickness, according to this definition is *temporary total disablement*. As a consequence, the victim must abstain from work and should receive medical care for speedy recovery. A person who has recovered from sickness in the ordinary medical sense but is still convalescing so that attendance to work may lead to relapse would be considered sick for the purpose of the scheme.

Cash benefit is provided in the event of sickness. This is often conditional as it is given on fulfilling certain contribution conditions and is usually limited in duration. Sickness is contingency which is usually protected on social insurance lines.

(b) Maternity

Maternity or childbirth is another contingency which is covered under social security schemes. Periodical payments to an insured woman in case of confinement or miscarriage or sickness arising out of pregnancy, confinement, premature birth of a child or miscarriage, such women being certified to be eligible for such payments by an authority specified in this behalf by the regulations is hereinafter referred to as maternity benefit.[23]

Cash benefit is paid to insured woman or even to the wife of a insured person in the event of confinement. This is usually payable for six week before and six weeks after the delivery at rates which vary from half of the wages to full wages. In some countries some additional lump sum allowances are also paid to enable the family to buy new clothings, toilet equipment and other things for the baby.

(c) Occupational Risks

The ILO defines this contingency as "traumatic injury or disease arising out of employment, not brought about deliberately or by serious or wilful misconduct of the victim, and resulting in temporary or total incapacity or death."[24] Thus occupational risks are two: Industrial Accidents and Occupational Diseases.

Cash Benefit is paid for accidents at work. This may be in the form of Temporary Disablement Benefit payable while the disablement lasts or it may be in the form of pension for life; the amount of benefit depends on the extent of Permanent Disablement. The benefit may also be in form of pensions for varying duration to dependants of the deceased insured person.

Occupational risks were formerly the responsibility of the employers alone. But they are now given social insurance protection under the modern schemes. In fact, this contingency is controllable to a great extent.

(d) Unemployment Benefit

Unemployment benefit is payable to able-bodied workers who are willing and available for employment but are unable to find any work. Entitlement to this benefit is also conditional on having paid certain contribution and is usually limited to certain number of days or weeks.

(e) Old Age and Invalidity Benefit

Pension is also payable in the event of invalidity, retirement or death of the employee. Invalidity and retirement pensions are payable to the worker and the survivorship pensions are payable to his dependants. For all these pensions, different qualifying conditions are attached.[25]

(f) Medical Care

In fact, public health is a public responsibility. Medical care is therefore generally organised by the State and financed by the general tax-payer. Apart from that, social security schemes also make a provision of medical care for the victims of sickness, employment hazards, invalidity and for the benefit of child bearing women.

Therefore, it is concluded that social security measures have a twofold significance for every developing country. They constitute an important step towards the goal of a welfare State by improving living and working conditions and affording the people protection against uncertainties of future. These measures are also important for every industrialisation plan, for not only do they enable workers to become more efficient, but they also reduce wastage arising from industrial disputes causing work stoppages. Lack of social security impedes production and prevents the formation of a stable and efficient labour force. Social security is, therefore, not a burden, but a wise investment which yields good dividends in the long run.[26] It is also obvious, that India has made significant progress in the field of social security, since independence.

Notes and Refereces

1. Dr. V.R. Bhattacharyya, Loc. Cit, (Auditor's Note, p. XI), Cited by V.G. Goswami, Labour and Industrial Laws, 1999, 7th edition, p. 13.
2. Government of India, Report of Committee on Labour Welfare, 1969, p. 255.
3. William Beverage: Report of Social Insurance and Allied Services, p. 6, Cited by S.C. Srivastava, 1985, p. 1.
4. *Ibid.*
5. Annie Ashley, The Social Policy of Bismark, Longman's Green and Co., London, 1912, p. 5.
6. N. Hasan, The Social Security System of India, 1972, pp. 32-33.
7. V.G. Goswami, Labour and Industrial Laws, 1999, 7th edition, p. 2.
8. N. Hasan, The Social Security System of India, 1972, p. 33.
9. V. George, Loc. Cit, p. 4, Cited by V.G. Goswami, Labour and Industrial Laws, 1999, 7th ediction, p. 3.
10. Report of the Second National Commission on Labour, 2002, 8.51.
11. Approaches to Social Security I.L.O. (Geneva 1942) p. 83.
12. N. Hasan, The Social Security System of India, 1972, pp. 2-3.
13. Social Security and Reconstruction in Canada, p. 16, Cited by V.G. Goswami, Labour and Industrial Laws, 1999, 7th edition, p. 4.
14. Encyclopaedia Americana, Vol. 25, p. 186.
15. Report of the First National Commission on Labour, 1969, p. 162.
16. Dr. V.R. Bhattacharyya, Some Aspects of Social Security Measures India, p. 2, Cited by V.G. Goswami, Labour and Industrial Laws, 1999, 7th edition p. 5.
17. N. Hasan, The Social Security System of India, 1972, p. 5.
18. Conventions and Recommendations, loc. cit. p. 528, Cited by V.G. Goswami, Labour and Industrial Laws, 1999, 7th edition, p. 10.
19. Approaches to Social Security, loc. cit. p. 84, Cited by V.G. Goswami, Labour and Industrial Laws, 1999, 7th edition, p. 10.
20. V.B. Singh, Loc. Cit. pp. 79-80, Cited by V.G. Goswami, Labour and Industrial Laws, 1999, 7th edition, p. 12.
21. Report of the First National Commission on Labour, 1969, p. 162.
22. Social Security : Principles; ILO, Geneva, 1944, p. 42.
23. Employees' State Insurance Act, Section 46 (b).
24. Social Security : Principles, p. 45, Cited by N. Hasan, The Social Security System of India,.1972, p. 12.
25. B.P. Tyagi, Labour Economics and Social Welfare, 2004, 9th edition, p. 489.
26. V.V. Giri, Loc, Cit, p. 271, Cited by V.G. Goswami, Labour and Industrial Laws, 1999, 7th edition, p. 13.

Social Security : Unorganised Sector

Social security is a basic need of all people regardless of employment in which they work and live. It is an important form of social protection. It should be begun with birth and should continue till death. In a general sense social security refers to protection extended by the society and State to its members to enable them to overcome various contingencies of life.[1]

The main risks or insecurity to which human life is responsible and in relation to which an organised society can afford relief to the helpless individuals are the incidents occuring right from childhood upto old age and death, which includes mainly sickness, invalidity due to maternity, accident and occupational diseases, unemployment, old age etc.

Though we have enacted good number of social security legislations to meet the mandate of our Constitution and provide a sort of protection to the people in case of various providential mishaps, the scope and coverage of these legislations is limited to hardly 9.4 percent of the total workforce, who are in the so-called organised sector, as per 1991

Census. But remaining 90.6% of the persons working in unorganised sectors such as the small and marginal farmers, the landless agricultural labours, the rural artisans, the handicrafts men and women, the fishermen and women, the salt workers, the hamals and the building and construction workers, etc., are deprived of protection under many social security legislations of the State. Thus majority of the workforce in the unorganised sectors are in an urgent need of a comprehensive social security protection which can be achieved by joint efforts of governmental and non-governmental organisations.[2]

1. NEED OF SOCIAL SECURITY FOR THE UNORGANISED SECTOR

The social security needs of the unorganised sector are extensive and varied whereas the funds available for the programmes are necessarily limited. These persons are the uncovered wage earners who work for very small employers. Their needs and characteristics are identical to those of the covered workers in the organised sector. Majority of the working people in the rural areas, especially in agriculture sector are deprived of any of the protections of the existing social security legislations. The small and marginal farmers who are badly hit by drought, flood, crop failures, epidemic diseases and others, such as loss of livestock etc. need some social assistance in the form of earning related programmes in the field of agriculture, animal husbandry etc., and also supply of seeds, pesticides and irrigation facilities. The other basic social security need in the rural areas is health care as they are more prone to various diseases.[3]

The element of income security and social protection—food, water, healthcare, childcare, shelter and education—need to be treated as basic entitlements of the workers and producers of the economy. They are entitled not only because they are citizens, but also because they are the main contributors to the wealth of the nation. Today, even without these entitlements they contribute their labour, skill and entrepreneurship to the economy. When provided with these entitlements, their productivity as well as their purchasing power will grow. They will add to the country's gross national product, strengthen the economy and help fight economic crises. On the other hand, if their economic contribution is not recognised and enhanced, if they continue to be treated as the recipients of safety net policies, they will continue to be poor beneficiaries, living constantly on welfare and subsidies. As structural adjustment proceeds, the entitlements of the organised sector are getting eroded, and the need for social security system is becoming more urgent and central to the success of structural adjustment programmes. Social security must contain at least healthcare (including maternity, injury) childcare, shelter and old age support that strengthen productivity and the economic security of the current workforce.[4]

2. OBSTACLES IN THE EXTENSION OF SOCIAL SECURITY

The main obstacle in the coverage of wage earners in tiny establishments is the formidable task of their identification and registration. This is more so in the cases of small artisans, fishermen, landless agricultural labours and other unprotected groups. The high cost involved in their coverage impels the social security administrations to shrink from the challenge. Further the number of persons in the unorganised sector is increasing due to Liberalization and Globalisation Policies. There is also a lack of vocal demand from the deprived population.

Social security measures for the unorganised sector labour are constrained by factors such as (i) lack of permanent or stable linkage between employer and employee that precludes schemes based on employer's contributions, (ii) low and unstable wages and lack of round-the-year employment which precludes schemes based on employee's contribution, and (iii) purely casual nature of employment which precludes benefits like sick leave, maternity leave etc.

Apart from this the weak economic capacity of rural communities, lack of adequate infrastructure of communication, illiteracy, lack of awareness about the social security measures, difficulty in determining wages and income and paucity of funds etc. are few important problems in the way of extension of social security to workers in unorganised sector.

3. STRATEGIES FOR EXTENSION OF SOCIAL SECURITY

Social protection for the poor and the deprived can be provided through a combination of measures including the expansion of the current social security schemes and the government funded social assistance programmes and the enlargement of the employment generations and poverty alleviation programmes.[5]

Apart from conventional social security, crop and livestock insurance schemes are a priority area of protection. Even though there are some crop insurance schemes existing in India, there is no awareness among the people who are often affected by crop failures etc. Further, establishment of more and more institutions of mutual benefit funds can provide an alternative system of social security for the unorganised sector particularly for the self-employed persons. The Panchayats and Nagarpalikas should be involved in administering social security programmes which helps to achieve effective targeting and accountable delivery of benefits, reduce overhead mobilize local resources and create a basis for community solidarity Further, the department of social justice welfare etc., must be made responsible to implement the social security schemes strictly and also be encouraged to ensure new schemes. In addition to these, the role of non-governmental organisations and social workers in implementation of schemes is more significant.

The needs of the people engaged in barely subsistence level activities such as semi-skilled craftsmen and vendors in urban areas and marginal farmers, fishermen, forestry workers and landless agricultural workers in rural areas require to be considered. Specifically with reference to their meagre incomes, the distinct social security measures are to be devised for them. Further, some measures are required to be taken to improve their conditions of work, health etc. Though many health centres have been established in many villages, the condition of health care is not upto mark due to lack of doctors, availability of drugs etc. Though many hospital buildings are constructed in rural areas, they are lying vacant without any medical staff and facilities. Therefore, Government must take immediate steps for recruitment of necessary staff and ensure the supply of drugs.[6]

Maternity benefits and provision of early childcare facilities are two related and important issues that need serious attention. At present, maternity benefit is available only in the organised sector, and very rarely in the unorganised sector. The provision for creches has not been enforced with strictness. As women need special attention, Apex Board/s should see that the scheme of social security includes maternity and early childcare, and are made a compulsory element in security measures in the unorganised sector.[7]

Provident fund benefits form the only range of financial support that workers enjoy on retirement. In the unorganised sector too, workers do need such a source of support. It is not that this facility is absent in the whole sector. Public Provident Fund for the self-employed and Employees Provident Fund for the workers should be made universal in the unorganised sector.[8]

Family benefits should mainly take the form of educational assistance to the children and dependants of the worker's family. Promotional measures like 'food for education' schemes should also be introduced.

The workers in the unorganised sector are facing a problem of housing. Due to low and uncertain income, they are unable to have their own shelter and as such are forced to live in huts etc. Though Government has evolved a housing scheme for poor, it has not yet reached millions of workers in the unorganised sector. Further, social assistance measures are inevitable to provide clothing and food for non-earning elderly without family support, unemployed handicapped persons, the deserted women and destitutes, agricultural workers and rural artisan and the effective programmes in the shape of poverty alleviation and employment generation be implemented properly.[9]

4. CONSTITUTIONAL BASIS FOR SOCIAL SECURITY IN INDIA

Constitution of India offers, protection and social security to all citizens of India. It is obvious that the workers in the unorganised sector are as much entitled to protection and welfare or social security as citizens in any other groups.

Preamble of Indian Constitution is the sole repository of social security measures and provides for establishment of Socialist State. According to Supreme Court of India, the principal aim of socialism is to eliminate inequality of income, status and standard of life and to provide a decent standard of life to the working people. Further it is designed to secure social, economic and political justice to all its citizens. Fundamental Rights include the right to equality,[10] the protection against discrimination,[11] the rights to freedom of speech and expression,[12] the rights to life and personal liberty,[13] protection against traffic in human beings, protection from forced labour,[14] and the rights of the child.[15]

The Directive Principles of State Policy (part IV of Constitution—Articles 36 to 51) spell out the concept of social security. Article 38 of the Constitution, requires the State to strive to promote welfare of the people by 'securing justice— social, economic and political and minimize inequalities in income and status between individuals, groups and regions.'

In the Judgement, Air India Statutory Corporation v. *United Labour Union,*[16] a three Judges of the Court has explained the concept of social justice in Article 38 as follows:

> The concept of 'social justice' consists of diverse principles essential for the orderly growth and development of personality of every citizen. "Social justice" is then an integral part of justice in the generic sense. Justice is the genus, of which "Social justice" is one of its species. Social justice is a dynamic devise to mitigate the sufferings of the poor, week dalits tribals and deprived sections of the society and so elevate them to the level of equality to live a life with dignity of person. Social justice is not a simple or single idea of a society but is an essential part of complex social change to relieve the poor etc., from handicaps, penury, to ward off distress and to make their life livable, for greater good of the society at large. The aim of social justice is to attain substantial degree of social, economic and political equality which is the legitimate expectation and constitutional goal. In a developing society likes ours, where there is vast gap of inequality in status and of opportunity, law is a catalyst, rubicon to the poor

etc. to reach the ladder of social justice. The Constitution, therefore, mandates the State to accord justice to all members of the society in all facets of human activity. The concept of social justice enables equality to flavour and enliven the practical content of life. Social justice and equality are complementary to each other so that both should maintain their vitality. Rule of law, therefore, is a potent instrument of social justice to bring about equality.

Articles 39 (a), (b) and (e) of the Constitution requires that the citizens have the right to adequate means of livelihood, that the material sources are so distributed as best to serve the common good, that the health and strength of workers and the tender age of children are not abused, and that citizens are not forced by economic necessity to enter avocations unsuited to their age or strength.

Article 41 requires that within the limits of its economic capacity and development, the State shall make effective provision for securing the right to work, to education and to public assistance in case of unemployment, old age, sickness and disablement, and in other cases of undeserved want. Article 42 requires that the State should make provision for securing just and human conditions of work and maternity relief. Article 43 requires that the State shall endeavour to secure work, a living wage, conditions of work ensuring a decent standard of life and full enjoyment of leisure and social and cultural opportunities. Article 47 requires that the State should regard the raising of the level of nutrition and the standard of living of its people, and improvement of public health, as among its primary duties.

Although these provisions are not enforceable in the courts of law, the Supreme Court of India has declared that they are nevertheless fundamental in the governance of the country and it is the duty of the State to apply them in making laws.

5. VARIOUS SCHEMES EVOLVED IN INDIA

Several schemes have been evolved in India through legislations and policies to provide social security to the workers in the unorganised sector. Some of the important schemes are *Integrated Rural Development Programme, Rural Group Life Insurance Scheme* introduced in 1995 in which insurance is available between ages 20-60 years for an assured amount of Rs. 5000 with a premium of Rs. 60 per annum. However the programmes in this scheme has not been very satisfactory all over the country and require revamping by undertaking effective publicity.[17]

Old Age Pension Scheme is another social security measure exists in almost all States in India, which is a monthly pension ranging between Rs. 50 to Rs. 100 and is applicable to the people whose income does not exceed the maximum slab prescribed. However, many of the old aged people who are eligible for pension under the scheme are not aware about the same and as such are deprived of the benefit. These schemes can be implemented properly through the local authorities by identifying the needy beneficiaries.[18]

The Life Insurance Corporation of India has introduced a variety of Group Insurance Schemes and saving schemes to cover members of co-operative societies and trade or occupational associations. Further the *National Agricultural Insurance Scheme* was launched in June 1999. The scheme provides insurance cover to all farmers, irrespective of the size of holdings and covers almost all crops. The premium rates are also very less and the scheme also has a provision of 50 percent subsidy on the premium, amount for small and marginal farmers. In case of failure of crops due to calamities such as cyclone, flood, hail-storm landslip etc. the affected person would be entitled to payment of insurance according to indemnity rates prescribed. The scheme provides for constitution of a separate organisation for its administration such as *Bharatiya Krishi Bhima Nigam (Indian Agricultural Insurance Corporation)*.[19]

Krishi Shramik Samajik Suraksha Yojana was launched in July, 2001 for giving social security benefit to agricultural labourers on hire in the age group of 18 to 60 years.[20]

The response to this scheme is very encouraging. This is a social security scheme providing for life-*cum*-accident insurance, money back and superannuation benefits. If this is to be extended to cover about 200 million agricultural workers, the Government exchequer will have to contribute Rs. 400 million per day. That amount to Rs. 14,600 crores per year.[21]

Shiksha Sahayog Yojana has been finalised for providing educational allowance of Rs. 100 per month to the children of parents living below the poverty line for their education from the 9th to 12th standard.[22]

Further, the Government of Orissa has introduced a scheme called *Orissa Unemployment Assistance Scheme, 1999* for providing livelihood to the educated unemployed whose family income does not exceed a prescribed limit per month and family must be in the below poverty line list. The rate of assistance is Rs. 200 per month payable for a maximum period of 3 years or till he or she is engaged in gainful employment whichever is earlier. The similar type of scheme may be implemented in other States also. The integrated housing scheme for beedi workers have been introduced by Government of India to provide housing facilities to beedi worker at a subsidised rate.[23]

The Jawahar Gram Samriddi Yojana has been launched streamlining and restructuring the Jawahar Rozgar Yojana which was existing earlier. The primary objective of this programme is creation of demand driven community village infrastructure including assets. It will also help create assets to enable the rural poor to increase opportunities for sustained development. The scheme will also generate supplementary employment for the unemployed poor in rural areas. The programme will be implemented with the help of village panchayat institutions and they are also empowered to execute work with approval of Gramsabhas. The cost of the programme is shared between Central and the State Governments in the ratio of 75:25. In case of Union Territories the total funding would be done by the centre.[24]

Swarnjayanti Gram Swarozgar Yojana (SGSY) was launched with effect from April 1, 1999 as a result of amalgamating certain erstwhile programmes *viz.*, Integrated Rural Development Programme (IRDP), Development of Women and Children in Rural areas (DWCRA), Training of Rural Youth for Self-Employment (TRYSEM), Million Wells Scheme (MWS) etc. into a single self-employment programme. It aims at promoting micro-enterprises and helping the rural poor into Self Help Groups (SHG). This scheme covers all aspects of self-employment like organisation of rural poor into SHG and their capacity building, training, planning of activity clusters, infrastructure development, financial assistance through bank credit and subsidy and marketing support etc. The scheme is being implemented as a Centrally Sponsored Scheme on a cost sharing ratio of 75:25 between the Centre and the States.[25]

Employment Assurance Scheme was started on October 2, 1993 for implementation in 1778 identified backward Panchayat Samitis of 257 districts situated in drought prone areas, desert areas, tribal areas and hill areas in which the revamped public distribution system was in operation. It was subsequently expanded by 1997-98 to all the 5448 rural Panchayat Samitis of the country. It was restructured in 1999-2000 to make it a single wage employment programme and implemented as a Centrally Sponsored Scheme on a cost sharing ratio of 75:25.[26]

Sampoorna Grameen Rojgar Yozana was launched w.e.f. September 2001, the scheme aims at providing wage employment in rural areas and also food security, along with the creation of durable community, social and economic assets. The scheme is being implemented on a cost sharing ratio of 75:25 between the Centre and States. The ongoing *Employment Assurance Scheme and Jawahar Gram Samridhi Yojana* would subsequently be fully integrated within the scheme with effect from April 1, 2002.[27]

Pradhan Mantri Gramodaya Yojana was introduced in 2000-01 with the objective of focussing on village level development in five critical areas, i.e. health, primary education, drinking water, housing and rural roads, with the overall objective of improving the quality of life of people in the rural areas.

(i) *Pradhan Mantri Gram Sadak Yojana* was launched on 25th December, 2000 with the objective of providing road connectivity through good all weather roads to all rural habitations with a population of more than 1000 persons by the year 2003 and those with a population of more than 500 persons by the year 2007. An allocation of Rs. 2500 crore has been provided for the scheme in 2001-02.

(ii) *Pradhan Mantri Gramodaya Yojana* is to be implemented on the pattern of Indra Awas Yojana with the objective of sustainable habitat development at the village level and to meet the growing housing needs of the rural poor.[28]

Samagra Awaas Yojana has been launched as a comprehensive housing scheme in 1999-2000 on pilot project basis in one block in each of 25 districts of 24 States and in one Union Territory with a view to ensuring integrated provision of shelter, sanitation and drinking water. The underlying philosophy is to provide for covergence of the existing housing, sanitation and water supply schemes with a special emphasis on technology transfer, human resource development and habitat improvement with people's participation.[29]

Food for Work Programme was initially launched w.e.f. February 2001 for five months and was further extended. The programme aims at augmenting food security through wage employment in the drought affected rural areas in eight States i.e. Gujarat, Chattisgarh, Himachal Pradesh, Madhya Pradesh, Maharashtra, Orissa, Rajasthan and Uttranchal. The workers are paid the balance of wages in cash, such that they are assured of the notified Minimum Wages. This programme stands extended upto March 31, 2002 in respect of notified "natural calamity affected Districts."[30]

Recently February 22, 2004, Social Security Scheme for Unorganised Sector Launched

In a pre poll bonanza for unorganised workers, Prime Minister Atal Bihari Vajpayee on sunday February 22, 2004 launched a social security scheme offering health insurance and old age pension to them and underlined the need to bring labourers under the organised sector.[31]

Vajpayee told a gathering of workers here that for the first time after independence, his government has chalked out a plan to insure lives of workers of unorganised sector.[32]

The Prime Minister, on a two day visit to his parliamentary constituency, Lucknow, the first after the dissolution of Lok Sabha, said his government fully appreciated the concerns and problems of unorganised workers and intended to solve them on priority basis.

Vajpayee said that rich do not need social security, but for the poor an umbrella of social security is must to protect them in case of accidents, ill-health or untimely death.

Asserting the NDA government was committed to provide social security to unorganised workers, he said the scheme would be managed by EPF Organisation.[33]

Initially the scheme would be launched in 50 select districts, including State capitals, he said adding "if it gets a good response, it will be implemented all over the country."

Vajpayee said the scheme would cover all workers in the uorganised sector drawing up to Rs. 650 per month as wages. It would be financed by contribution from workers at the rate of Rs. 50 per month in the 18-35 age group and Rs. 100 per month in the 36-50 age group.[34]

Contribution from the employers would be Rs. 100 per month and the government contribution would be 1.16 per cent of the monthly wage of workers or up to Rs. 250 per month, Vajpayee said.

He said a worker would get a pension of Rs. 500 per month on retirement, adding in case of untimely death, family members of a worker would get Rs. 1.25 lakh plus pension of Rs. 500 per month. In case of hospitalisation, a worker would get Rs. 30,000 as reimbursement and family members Rs. 50 per day for 15 days, he added.[35]

Beside this, in November 14, 2004, Prime Minister Manmohan Singh launched the *National Food for Work Programme* at village Aloor in Ranga Reddy District in Andhra Pradesh. NFFWP will provide additional supplementary wage employment in the identified 150 most backward districts of the country. NFFWP is a 100% centrally sponsored scheme. The programme will focus on water conservation, drought proofing, flood control, rural development and rural connectivity.[36]

In year 2005, various Schemes has been Launched

Rajiv Gandhi Shramik Kalyan Yojana was launched with effect from 1 April, 2005, under the scheme, insured workers who lose their jobs after having contributed to the ESI scheme for five years or more shall be entitled to an "unemployment allowance" in cash. The allowance equivalent to about 50 percent of their wages, will be valid for a maximum period of 6 months.

The Government has announced this ambitious scheme to provide social security to its eight million employees, and their families insured under the Employees State Insurance Corporation.[37]

Announcing the scheme in the Lok Sabha Labour Minister K. Chandra Sekhar Rao said this was the first time that an unemployment-related benefit scheme was being launched in the country.

Rao added that those availing of the 'unemployment allowance' (and their families) would also be eligible to receive medical care from ESI dispensaries and hospitals. This medical benefit will extend to 30 million family members of ESIC workers.[38]

The ESIC proposes to meet the expenditure of the scheme out of its existing resources. The minister said Rs. 300 crore would be provided in accordance with the rules under the ESI Act for this purpose.

The Minister said the "highly labour friendly" scheme was being launched in pursuance of the UPA's CMP. Rao explained that there are often situations when industrial units and other establishments were closed down for a variety of reasons. During such period of unemployment and till they were able to find alternative employment the economic and social condition of workers and their families became highly vulnerable. The scheme had been floated to provide a sort of a safety net for such workers, the labour minister said.[39]

Recognising the importance of health in the process of economic and social development and improving the quality of life of people, Prime Minister Dr. Manmohan Singh has launched the *National Rural Health Mission in 2005* to carry out necessary architectural correction in the basic health care delivery system. The Mission adopts a synergic approach by relating health to determinants of good health viz. of nutrition, sanitation, hygiene and safe drinking water. It also aims at mainstreaming the Indian systems of medicine to facilitate health care. The plan of Action includes increasing public expenditure on health, reducing regional imbalance in health infrastructure, pooling resources, integration of organizational structures, optimization of health manpower, decentralization and district management of health programmes, community participation and ownership of assets, induction of management and financial personnel into district health system, and operationalising Community Health Centers into functional hospitals meeting Indian Public Health Standards in each Block of the country.[40]

The goal of the Mission is to improve the availability of and access to quality healthcare by people, especially for those residing in rural areas, the poor women and children. This is an ambitious and new concept of the UPA government as enshrined in its National Common Minimum Programme.

The Mission covers the entire country but gives a special focus on 18 states, which have weak health infrastructure and demographic indicators. The project is basically a strategy for integrating the on-going vertical programmes of Health and Family Welfare. It adopts a sector-wide approach and aims at systematic reforms to enable efficiency in health service delivery. It also subsumes key national programmes like Reproductive and Child Health-II Project, the National Disease Control Programmes and the Integrated Disease Surveillance Project. It will also enable the mainstreaming of AYUSH-Ayurvedic, Yoga, Unani, Siddha and Homeopathy system of health.

While providing a broad framework for operationalisation, the Mission lists a set of core strategies to meet its goals like decentralized village and district level health planning and management, appointment of female Accredited Social Health Activists (ASHA) to facilitate access to health services. The government hopes that with ASHA, the healthcare services are finally at the doorstep of every village household and this is expected to transform the health status of the village society and the Nation.[41]

The Uttar Pradesh Chief Minister Mulayam Singh Yadav, launched *'Bhoomi Sena Scheme'* in Oct. 2005. This scheme is aimed at accomplishing the twin objectives of creating productive employment and utilising the barren land for increasing agricultural growth. The scheme will guarantee a minimum 100 day employment to landless farmers and labourers, besides small and marginal farmers.

A total of Rs. 100 crore will be spent in all 70 districts under the scheme, which also foresees creating 110 lakh man days, through an army of unemployed, each one of whom will be paid an assured daily wage of Rs. 58 for a period of two years, the total span of the scheme.[42]

"Tamil Nadu Chief Minister's Farmers Security Scheme", has been launched Oct. 2005. This scheme would benefit 86 lakh from workers and 51 lakh small and marginal farmers in the state. The Chief Minister Jaylalithaa said all small and marginal farmers and agricultural labour between the age of 18 and 65 years were eligible to enrol in the scheme,. which would cost Rs. 250 crores per annum. Though the subscription for the social security scheme was Rs. 10 a member, the Government would pay it for them which would cost the exchequer Rs. 13.75 crores.[43]

The registered members were entitled to various benefits, including an accident death assistance of Rs. 1 lakh to the members of the bereaved family Rs. 1 lakh for permanent disability in accidents, Rs. 10,000 for natural death, Rs. 3000 in case of marriage of male members and Rs. 5000 in case of female members in the family and Rs. 2500 to meet funeral expenses of the deceased member.[44]

These are some of the important social security schemes evolved in India to protect the interest of the workers in the unorganised sector.

Apart from constitutional mandate, social security for all is considered as a basic Human Right under the Universal Declaration of Human Rights. Every member nation of U.N.O. must strive to further and promote this basic right. As the study on the subject of social security: Unorganised sector reveals, though many schemes and policies have been evolved both at Central and State level to achieve the said object, the result is not so satisfactory because of non-implementation of the schemes properly. Even new schemes is launched in year 2004 and 2005 if these schemes are not properly implemented, the same with the other schemes. To make these schemes, effective, both governmental and non-governmental organisations must be encouraged. Further more and more social assistance programme be evolved because in case of social insurance schemes the workers in the unorganised sector are unable to contribute regularly due to uncertainty of income etc. But at the same time there must be a proper control and check to prevent misuse of the social assistance programmes.

Notes and References

1. Suresh V. Nadagoudar, "Social Security for Workers in the Unorganised Sector", Cochin University Law Review, 2002, Vol. XXVI, p. 191.
2. *Ibid.*
3. *Ibid.* p. 193.
4. Report of the Second National Commission on Labour, 2002 pp. 741-742.
5. Suresh V. Nadagoudar, "Social Security for Workers in the Unorganised Sector", Cochin University Law Review, 2002 Vol. XXVI, p. 194.
6. *Ibid.* p. 195.
7. Report of the Second National Commission on Labour, 2002, Vol. I, Part-I, 7.450.
8. *Ibid.*
9. Suresh V. Nadagoudar, "Social Security for Workers in the Unorganised Sector", *Cochin University Law Review*, 2002 Vol. XXVI, p. 195.
10. Article 14 says that : The State shall not deny to any person equality before the law or equal protection of the laws within the territory of India.
11. Article 15(1) says that: The state is prohibited to discriminate between citizens on the grounds only of religion, race, caste, sex, place of birth or any of them.
12. Article 19(1) says that : All citizens shall have the right to freedom of speech and expression.
13. Article 21 says that: No person shall be deprived of his life or personal liberty except according to procedure established by law.
14. Article 23 provides that : Traffic in human being and begar and other similar forms of forced labour are prohibited and any contravention to this provision shall be offence punishable in accordance with law.
15. Article 24 provides that : No child below the age of fourteen years shall be employed to work in any factory or mine or engaged in any other hazardous employment.
16. AIR 1997 SC 645.
17. Suresh V. Nadagoudar, "Social Security for Workers in the Unorganised Sector", *Cochin University Law Review*, 2002 Vol. XXVI, p. 196.
18. *Ibid.*
19. *Ibid.*
20. B.P. Tyagi, Labour Economics and Social Welfare, 2004, 9th edition, p. 739.
21. Report of the Second National Commission on Labour, 2002, Vol. I, Part-I, p. 686.
22. B.P. Tyagi, Labour Economics and Social Welfare, 2004, 9th ediction, p. 739.

23. Suresh V. Nadagoudar, "Social Security for Workers in the Unorganised Sector, *Cochin University Law Review*, 2002, Vol. XXVI, p. 197.
24. *Ibid.*
25. B.P. Tyagi, Labour Economics and Social Welfare, 2004, 9th edition, p. 736.
26. *Ibid.*, pp. 736-737.
27. *Ibid.*, p. 737.
28. *Ibid.*, p. 737.
29. *Ibid.*, p. 738.
30. *Ibid.*, p. 738.
31. *The Hindustan Times*, February 23, 2004.
32. *Ibid.*
33. *Ibid.*
34. *Ibid.*
35. *Ibid.*
36. *Employment Newspaper*, 30 April - 6 May, 2005.
37. *The Hindustan Times*, March 18, 2005.
38. *Ibid.*
39. *Ibid.*
40. V. Mohan Rao, "Quality Healthcare for Rural Poor", *Employment Newspaper*, 11-17 June, 2005.
41. *Ibid.*
42. *The Hindu*, October 31, 2005.
43. *The Hindu*, Oct. 6, 2005.
44. *Ibid.*

Legislations Relating to Unorganised Sector

We have many labour laws in our Statute books. All of them do not cover workers engaged in unorganised/informal sector. All of them are not applicable, and were not mean to be applicable to the employments in the unorganised sector. Some are applicable. But none of the laws that form the base of the social security system covers the whole unorganised sector. There are laws that apply wholly or partly to this sector.[1] These laws are: *The Factories Act, 1948, The Minimum Wages Act, 1948, The Equal Remuneration Act, 1976, The Payment of Wages Act, 1936, The Industrial Disputes Act, 1947, The Workmen Compensation Act, 1923, The Payment of Gratuity Act, 1972, etc.* which are applicable to the workers in the unorganised sector where there is an identifiable employer-employee relationship. In some of the employments or avocations, contractors are engaged, and this results in a situation in which the principal employer does not come into the picture such an in building/ construction activity, beedi rolling, mining (particularly stone mining) or quarrying, and various other occupations. These workers are sometimes covered under more than one law e.g. the *Contract Labour (Regulation and Abolition) Act, 1970*, as well as under one specific law or another like *Beedi and Cigar Workers (Conditions of Employment) Act, 1966, Building and other Construction Workers' (Regulation of Employment and Conditions of Service) Act, 1996* etc.

Inspite of the existence of these beneficial laws, the benefits and facilities prescribed under these laws are denied to them in most cases.[2] We have no escape from concluding that more than 90% of our workforce do not enjoy the minimum protection and security that they need. This is a situation which should shame all those who talk of care and commitment to the rights and welfare of labour, as well as all those who bear responsibility for ensuring the rights and welfare of our people, in particular, the overwhelming majority of our people who are in the labour force. Hence there is strong need and necessity to extend the facilities to the workers in the unorganised sector.

1. THE FACTORIES ACT, 1948

The Factories Act, 1948 is designed to protect workers in the factories. The Act has undergone various amendments and was last updated in 1987. The main object of the Act was to ensure adequate safety measures and to promote the health and safety of the workers employed in factories. Various Sections of the Act deal with benefits and welfare facilities and health, safety and hygiene inside the factory premises.

Provisions regarding health of the workers relate mainly to cleanliness, disposal of wastes and affluents, ventilation, control of temperature, elimination of dust and fumes, artificial humidification, overcrowding, lighting, drinking water facilities, latrines, urinals and spittons.[3] Besides, every factory has to make effective arrangements to provide and maintain a sufficient supply of wholesome drinking water for all workers employed therein;[4] and where 250 or more workers are working, employers are required to provide cool drinking water in hot weather.[5]

Provisions regarding safety of workers relate to the fencing of machinery, easing of new machinery, testing and examination of appliances and plants such as hoists, lifts, cranks, chains and pressure plants, supply of safety appliances to workers, precautions against dangerous fumes and in case of fire etc.[6] The Act also lays down the conditions under which young persons may be employed on dangerous machines and prohibits the employment of women and children for pressing cotton-opener is at work.[7]

Provision regarding welfare facilities cover such items as washing facilities for storing and drying clothes, facilities for sitting, first aid appliances, canteens in case of factories employing over 250 workers, suitable shelters or rest rooms, lunch rooms.[8] The Act also grants power to State Governments to make rules requiring the representatives of workers in any factory to be associated with management in regard to welfare arrangement of the workers.[9]

The implementation of the Act is under the jurisdiction of the State Governments. It is enforced through the Factory Inspectorates. Any worker can complain to the Inspector about conditions inside the factory, and the source from which the complaint has come is not supposed to be disclosed. Unfortunately, the implementation mechanism of the Act is unsatisfactory. Each factory inspector has more than a thousand factories under him. This infrastructural facilities available to him are totally inadequate.

This Act, in its updated form, has a very broad definition of 'worker'. However, contract and *ad hoc* workers do not get the benefits given to permanent workers. It imposes restrictions on employment of women during the night, especially the period between 7.00 p.m. to 6.00 a.m. There are also restrictions of daily working hours for men and women in factories. Sections 23 and 27 of the Factories Act prohibit women from handling dangerous devices. However, all these provisions are not applied in practice for a section of the workers. Moreover, the Act is applicable only to manufacturing units, organised as factories. The provisions of this Act do not apply to the vast masses of workers in the unorganised sector employed in smaller manufacturing units and other sectors.

2. CONTRACT LABOUR (REGULATION AND ABOLITION) ACT, 1970

Contract Labour (Regulation and Abolition) Act, 1970 regulates the employment of contract labour in certain establishments and provides for its abolition in certain circumstances. The Act is applicable if the principal employer engages twenty or more contract workers in an establishment. The contractor who employs twenty or more workers in his contract work will be covered under *The Contract Labour (Regulation and Abolition) Act, 1970.* The Act provides for the registration of all establishment of Principal Employers and licensing of all contractors. There is a special provision for the abolition of the contract system if certain conditions are met, like the nature of jobs being of perennial nature and connected with the core business of the principal employer.[10]

There are a number of provisions in the Act for the welfare and safety of contract labour.[11] There shall be provided and maintained by the contractor so as to be readily accessible during all working hours a first aid box equipped with the prescribed contents at every place where contract labour is employed by him.[12] For regulating its implementation, certain registers, records, returns etc. are to be maintained by the principal employers and contractors.

Penalties have been prescribed for those who violate the law. This Act is meant for unorgnised labour. But its scope is very limited. The limitation in the law are such that the contractor stands to gain if he engages less than twenty workers. This provision provides a loophole for all manner of manipulations by employers and contractors. Therefore, it can be seen that the coverage that this Act provides is far from satisfactory.

3. BEEDI AND CIGAR WORKERS (CONDITIONS OF EMPLOYMENT) ACT, 1966

Beedi and Cigar Workers (Conditions of Employment) Act, 1966 is an Act that provides for the welfare of the workers in Beedi and Cigar establishments, and regulates the conditions of their work and related matters. The Act provides for licensing of all industrial premises where beedi or cigar or both are made. It provides for cleanliness and ventilation and prohibits overcrowding of the premises. Every industrial premises shall be kept clean and free from effuvia arising from any drain, privy or other nuisance and shall also maintain such standard of cleanliness including white washing, colour washing vanishing or painting, as may be prescribed.[13] For the purpose of preventing injury to the health of the persons working therein, every industrial premises shall maintain such standard of lighting, ventilation and temperature as may be prescribed.[14] No room in any industrial premises shall be overcrowded to an extent injurious to the health of the persons employed therein.[15]

The welfare measures that it provides for includes arrangements for drinking water, latrines and urinals, washing facilities, creches, first aid and canteens, working conditions prescribe working hours, wages for overtime, interval for rest, spread over, weekly holidays and annual leave with wages. No child shall be required or allowed to work in any industrial premises.[16] No women or young person shall be required or allowed to work in any industrial premises except between 6 a.m. and 7 p.m.[17]

The employees who are given raw-material by an employer or a contractor for making beedi and cigars at home are covered under the Act. Persons not employed by an employer or a contractor but working with the permises of, or under agreement with the employer or contractor are also covered. Section 43 of the Act does not cover the self-employed persons in the beedi and cigar making industry. If the owner or occupier of the dwelling or house is not the employee of an employer, and carries on any beedi and cigar making work as self-employment, the person is not covered under the Act.

4. PLANTATION LABOUR ACT, 1951

This Act regulates, for the first time, the condition of work of plantation workers and provides for their welfare. Though, in the first instance, it applies only to tea, coffee, rubber and cinnamon plantations, the State Governments have been empowered to extend the provisions of the Act to other plantations with the approval of the Central Government.

The Act fixes 54 hours of work of a week for adults and 40 hours of work a week for adolescent and children;[18] it prohibits the employment of children, under 12 years of age and night work for women and children between the hours 7 p.m. and 6 a.m.[19] and requires medical examination of young persons below 18 years of age. It also provides for leave with wages for an adult at the rate of one day for every 15 days of work.[20]

The Plantations Labour Act, 1951 makes provision for health and welfare of the plantation workers. It makes provision for housing, medical aid, recreational and educational facilities in accordance with the rules framed by State Governments. The workers are entitled to sickness allowance and maternity allowance under the prescribed conditions.[21] The planters, who are employing more than 150 workers are required to provide and maintain canteens.[22]

The creches are to be maintained in plantations where more than 50 women workers are employed.[23] The employers are also required to make effective arrangements for supply of wholesome drinking water.[24] Welfare officers are to be appointed where more than 300 workers are employed, subject to State Governments rules.[25] Provision has also been made requiring every employer to provide and maintain for every worker and his family residing in the plantation, the necessary housing accommodation.[26]

In plantation, the position is equally unsatisfactory though some of the better organised estates have provided a high standard of welfare amenities.

5. BUILDING AND OTHER CONSTRUCTION WORKERS' (REGULATION OF EMPLOYMENT AND CONDITIONS OF SERVICE) ACT, 1996

Building and Other Construction Workers' (Regulation of Employment and Conditions of Service) Act, 1996 is an Act to regulate the employment and conditions of service of building and other construction workers and to provide for their safety, health and welfare and other incidental matters. The Act applies to every building or other construction work establishment, which employs or had employed ten or more workers. It covers all Central and State government establishments. The special feature of the Act is that it covers all private residential buildings if the cost of construction is more than Rupees ten lakhs.

Registration of the establishment is compulsory, and no establishment without registration can employ any building or construction worker. A worker between 18 and 60 years has to be registered to become eligible for the benefits of the Act. He/She must have put in at least 90 days of work in the previous year to acquire eligibility for registration. Every registered workers gets an identity card, and work entries are made in the card. The worker remains a beneficiary up to the age of 60, and for the year when he/she puts in at least 90 days of work.

A fund has to be created with the revenue from a cess collected from the employers, and contributions by the workers. Benefits include assistance in cases of accident, payment of pension, house building loans, assistance for group insurance schemes, education of children, maternity benefits for female beneficiaries and so on. There are provisions for regulating working hours, welfare measures and other conditions of service. The law also prescribes safety and health measures, and all other precautions that are required for safe working, e.g. safety devices for installation work, demolition work, excavation, underground construction, handling measures, proper ladders, ropes and fencing etc. Inspections and penalties are provided for.

In actual practice, the provisions of this Act are beneficial only to the skilled workers and those who work continuously in the industry. Unskilled workers, who do not work with a construction establishment continuously, may not get the benefits available under the Act. It will not be possible for those unskilled, uneducated and purely casual workers to make regular, timely contributions to fund as per the provisions of the law.

6. DOCK WORKERS' (REGULATION OF EMPLOYMENT) ACT, 1948

The Act and the scheme are social legislation enacted for the purpose of the welfare of the dock workers. The Act *inter alia,* empowers the Central Government in the case of major ports, and the State Governments in the case of other ports, to frame for the registration of dock workers in order to ensure greater regularity of employment. Such schemes may provide for the satisfactory regulation of a variety of subjects connected with the conditions of life and work of the dock workers, such as their recruitment, conditions of employment training and welfare. Provision has been made in the Act for the setting up of training and welfare centres.

Provision has also been made in the Act for the setting up of a tripartite Advisory Committee consisting of not more than 15 members representing government, dock workers and their employers in equal proportion, to advise government in the administration of the Act or any scheme formulated thereunder.[27] Provision has also been made for the appointment of Inspectors for the purpose of the Act.[28]

Under the Act, Dock workers Regulation of Employment Schemes have been framed for dock workers in the ports of Bombay, Calcutta and Madras. Tripartite Dock Labour Boards have been appointed in these ports.[29]

The Dock Workers' (Regulation of Employment) Act, 1948 was amended in March 1962. The main provision in the amending Act relates to: (a) the registration of employers and charging a registration fee from them; (b) the constitution of Dock Labour Boards to Administer the Scheme; (c) the appointment of auditors; and (d) the representation of shipping interest on the Dock Worker's Advisory Committees.[30]

In respect of ports and dock, one committee, appointed by the Government of India, 1964, came to the conclusion that facilities available to the workers were inadequate and even those limited facilities were not maintained properly nor were they used by the workers with the needed care.

7. MINIMUM WAGES ACT, 1948

The Minimum Wages Act, 1948 is the most important legislation that has been enacted for the benefit of unorganised labour. It was enacted for fixing, reviewing and revising the minimum rates of wages in the scheduled employments where workers are engaged in the unorganised sector. Under Section 3 of the Act, the appropriate Government has been empowered to fix the minimum rates of wages payable to employees employed in the scheduled employments and in an employment added to either part I or part II of the schedule by notification under section 27.

The Minimum Wages Act is meant to ensure that the market forces, and the laws of demand and supply are not allowed to determine the wages of workmen in industries where workers are poor, vulnerable, unorganised and without bargaining power. The minimum rates of wages are fixed, keeping in view the minimum requirements of a family, and wages at these rates are to be paid by all employers irrespective of their capacity to pay.

The appropriate Government is empowered under Section 13 of the Act to fix the number of hours per day. Besides provision has been made for weekly holidays and payment of overtime wages etc. in regard to any scheduled employment in respect of which minimum rates of wages have been fixed under this Act.

The Act helps unorganised workers who are working in the scheduled employments. But nearly 60% of the workforce in the unorganised sector is self-employed or home-based. Thus, they remain outside the purview of *The Minimum Wages Act, 1948,* although they constitute the majority in the sector.

8. PAYMENT OF WAGES ACT, 1936

The Payment of Wages Act, 1936 regulates the payment of wages to certain classes of employed persons. The main purpose of the Act is to ensure regular and prompt payment of wages and to prevent the exploitation of wage earners by prohibiting arbitrary fines and deduction from wages. The Act was subsequently amended in 1957, 1962, 1964, 1967, 1976 and 1982 in order to extend its various provisions and coverage. By virtue of the amending Act of 1982 the wage limit was raised to cover persons drawing less than Rs. 1600 per month.

It ensures the correct and timely payment of wages and ensures that no unauthorized or arbitrary deductions are made. This Act applies to persons employed in factories, mines, oil fields, railways and various other establishments specified in the Act. However because of the wage limit of Rs. 1600 for the purpose of applicability of the Act 95% of the unorganised workers are excluded from the coverage of the Act.

The Act is not applicable to self-employed/home-based workers, as they are not persons employed in the category of establishments mentioned in the Act. It does not, therefore protect a large number of workers in the unorganised sector.

9. THE MINES ACT, 1952

The Mines Act, 1952, was enacted to amend and consolidate the law relating to the regulation of labour and safety in mines. The Act extends to the whole of India and it aims at providing for safe as well as proper working conditions in mines and certain amenities to workers employed therein. Elaborate provisions have been made in the Act for safeguarding the health and safety of workers and for promoting their welfare. In every mine where more than 150 persons are employed, a first aid room under the charge of medical and nursing staff is to be provided and maintained.[31] In every mine effective arrangements shall be made to provide and maintain at suitable points conveniently situated a sufficient supply of cool and wholesome drinking water for all persons employed therein.[32]

For the safety of the workers there are provisions for conveyance and use of explosives; safety of the roads and working places in mines; inspection of working conditions and sealed off fire areas in mines, ventilation, lighting and fencing. Preventing measures against inflammable gases are to be taken. Provision has also to be made for adequate safeguard of persons working underground and for periodical examination of shafts, inclines and outlets to the surface.

Provision has been made in regard to hours and limitation of employment. No person shall be allowed to work in a mine on more than six days in anyone week.[33] No adult employed above ground in a mine shall be required or allowed to work for more than forty eight hours in any week or for more than nine hours in any day.[34] Where in a mine a person works above ground for more than nine hours in any day or works below ground for more than eight hours in any day, or works for more than forty eight hours in any week whether above ground or below ground, he shall in respect of such overtime work be entitled to wages at the rate of twice his ordinary rate of wages, the period of overtime work being calculated on a daily basis or weekly basis, whichever is more favourable to him.[35]

Though comprehensive, the Act did not break new ground, since it paid more attention to safety measures and provisions of medical facilities in the nature of first aid rather than any comprehensive medical aid to workers.

10. WORKMEN'S COMPENSATION ACT, 1923

The Workmen's Compensation Act, 1923 provides for the payment of compensation to workmen for injuries sustained in accidents. After the amendments effected in 1995, the Act has *4 Schedules. Schedule I* provides a list of injuries with percentage of disablement (loss of earning capacity). If the injury is not a scheduled injury, the loss of earning capacity has to be proved by evidence. The majority of the workers who are not insured under the ESI scheme are covered under *The Workmen's Compensation Act.* The Act does not apply to those who are employed in occupations enlisted in the *Schedule II.* Nor is relief available if the injury has taken place when the injured worker was not actually engaged in discharging duties related to the employer's trade or business. The employer is liable to provide monetary compensation to the worker or dependent in case of death or disablement provided it occurs 'out of and in the course of employment'. An occupational disease listed in *Schedule III* of the Act is also accepted as an accident that occurred while on duty. The burden of proving that the accident arose out of employment is upon the worker.

The method of claiming compensation for disability is so long and torturous that one rarely gets the compensation to which one is entitled by law. Any qualified medical practitioner can certify the case, and the victim can file a claim in the court of the workmens compensation commissioner with a copy to the employer. The workmens compensation commissioner decides the case, and the revenue department recovers the amount of compensation. But workers who are in the *unorganised sector,* often find it very difficult to prove who is their employer, and as a result cases are prolonged, and often workers die without receiving any compensation.

The Workmen's Compensation (Amendment) Act, 2000 that came into effect in December 2000 provides for compensation even to casual workers. The minimum amount of compensation for death has been enhanced from Rs. 50,000 to Rs. 80,000 and for total disablement from Rs. 60,000 to Rs. 90,000. The ceiling on monthly wage/salary reckoned for determining the compensation amount has also been increased from Rs. 2000 to Rs. 4000. The amount of funeral expenses payable has also been increased to Rs. 2500 from Rs. 1000.

11. INTER-STATE MIGRANT WORKMEN (REGULATION OF EMPLOYMENT AND CONDITIONS OF SERVICE) ACT, 1979

The vast majority of migrant workers fall in the unorganised sector. Workers are recruited from various parts of a State through contractors or agents commonly known as 'sardars', generally for work outside the State wherever construction projects are available. This system lends itself to various abuses. The promises that contractors make at the time of recruitment about higher wages and regular and timely payments are not usually kept. No working hours are fixed for these workers and they have to work all days in the week under extremely bad, often intolerable working conditions in inhospitable environments. The provisions of various labour laws are not observed, and migrant workers are often subjected to various forms of malpractices.

The Inter-State Migrant Workmen (Regulation of Employment and Conditions of Service) Act, 1979 was enacted to regulate the employment and conditions of service of inter-state migrant workers.

The benefits include non-discrimination in wage rates, holidays, hours of work and other conditions of work for inter-State migrant workers in relation to local workers. They are eligible for a non-refundable Displacement Allowance equal to 50% of their monthly wages in addition to the wages.[36] A journey allowance, equal to rail fares both ways, is to be paid by the contractor with wages during the period of journeys.[37] Other provisions include regular payment of wages, equal pay for equal work to both men and women workers and provisions for suitable conditions of work, suitable residential accommodation, adequate medical facilities and adequate protective clothing and equipment.[38] In case of accidents, there is a provision to ensure intimation to the authorities of both the States (Home State and Host State) and to the next of kin.

"Inter-State migrant workman" is defined in Section 2(e) of the Act. It means 'any person who is recruited by or through a contractor in one State under an agreement or other arrangement for employment in an establishment in another State, whether with or without the knowledge of the principal employer in relation to such establishment'. According to this definition, we find that all migrant workers (who are generally unorganised workers) are not inter-State migrant workers as defined by the law, and cannot, therefore, enjoy the benefits of the ISMW Act. To prove in Court that the Act is applicable is very difficult, as employers deny that workmen were recruited from another State (Home State) by any of their contractors. They often contend that the workers were recruited from nearby places within the State where the industry is located. Thus, the Act is only of very limited benefit to workers in the unorganised sector.

It looks anomalous that unorganised workers can receive the limited benefits of the existing labour laws only if they happen to work for employers, in other words, if there is an employer-employee relationship. None of these labour laws can provide protection to the vast majority of unorganised workers who are self-employed or home-based or to other workers who are employed in enterprises where the number of employees does not reach the threshold prescribed by the Acts.

12. THE UNORGANISED SECTOR WORKERS (EMPLOYMENT AND WELFARE) BILL, 2003

The unorganised sector accounts for over 90% of our workforce. Their percentage is likely to increase. They are as entitled to protection and welfare/security as workers in the organized sector, who are often described today as the privileged sector of the workforce. The laws that exist today hardly touch the workforce in the unorganised sector. It is therefore, necessary to enact new legislation to cover workers in this sector. There is a wide variety of employments in this sector. Conditions vary, levels of organisation vary. The nature of the relations with employers vary. There is an expanding sector of those who are self-employed, or are on contract, and work from homes. It is difficult to have separate laws for each employment. This will only result in endless multiplication of laws, and oversight of one or the other of the employments. The answer therefore lies in one Umbrella legislation that covers whatever is basic and common, and leaves room for supplementary legislation or rules where specific areas demand special attention.

The Umbrella legislation for the unorganised sector workers' employment and welfare should be seen as an enabling legislation that will lead to the growth of the economy, improve the quality of employment, provide a decent life to the workers and integrate them with the growing opportunities in the country. The essence of the proposed Umbrella legislation is removal of poverty of the working population of India through improving their productivity, quality of work, enhancing income earning abilities and increasing its bargaining power.[39]

The Unorganised Sector Workers (Employment and Welfare) Bill, 2003 is the reaction of the Indian ruling classes, to the present crisis. The Bill is the logical outcome of the Second National Labour Commission's recommendations. An Act to consolidate and amend the laws relating to the regulation of employment and welfare of workers in the unorganised sector in India and to provide protection and social security to these workers.

The objectives of the Act are : (1) to obtain recognition of all workers in the unorganised sector, (2) to ensure a minimum level of economic security, (3) to ensure a minimum level of social security, (4) to expedite removal of the poverty of these workers through their work, protecting their means of employment and income, (5) to ensure future opportunities for children by progressive elimination of child labour, (6) to ensure equal opportunities of work, for men and women workers.

The Unorganised Sector Workers Bill, 2003 consists of seven parts. *First part* deals with Short Title, Extent and Commencement, Objectives of the Act and Definitions. *Second part* deals with Constitution of Boards, Functioning of Board through Worker Facilitation Centres, Functions of the Central Board, State Board, Employment Based Boards, District Boards, and State Board in relation to self-employed workers. *Part third* provides provisions relating to Functions of WFC and Registration, Identity Card, Funds, Investment of funds, Ceiling on administrative costs. *Part fourth* deals with Workers Organisations. *Part fifth* provides provisions relating to Minimum Wages, Allowances, Social security, Health and Safety, Holidays and General provisions. *Part sixth* deals with Education, Training and Skill Development. *Part seventh* deals with provisions relating to Registers and Records, Grievance redressal, Framing of Rules and schemes.

Section 4 (1) of the Bill provides that "Unorganised Sector Workers' Central Board" refers to the Central level apex board. It will be constituted by the Central Government for the effective implementation of the provisions of this Act and to co-ordinate functions under this Act at the national level. Section 4 (2) provides that "State Board" means the State level apex Board. These may be called "(name of the state)..... Unorganised Sector Workers Board". The concerned State Government will constitute the State Board. The State Board will coordinate functioning at the State or Union territory level of other employment-specific State Welfare Board.

Section 12 of the Bill provides that each worker on registration will be given a registration number and a permanent identification number and a permanent identity card or work card on payment of a registration fee. It shall have the details of his person, name, address, work wages/income social security entitlements and his photographs. The permanent identification number will be valid all over India. The State Board will decide the system of raising funds in consultation with its subordinate lower boards for different classes of worker.[40] The Central and State Board will raise funds by way of contribution, cess, assistance, grant from Government through budget allocation or donations from employment providers, private sector, workers and other legally permitted sources. The Central and Board and State Boards shall plan management of funds efficiently.[41]

Section 17 of the Bill provides provisions relating to minimum wage these are (1) The worker shall receive minimum economic returns or minimum wages for his work as prescribed by law. (2) The State Board shall have the right to recommend to the State Government concerned minimum wages of the operations and avocations not covered under other laws, and where there is employer-employee relationship. (3) There shall be a minimum wage. (4) There shall be no gender discrimination in deciding wages or benefits. (5) The Central or State Boards and their appointed machinery shall perform the implementations of minimum wage. (6) Non-payment of minimum wage shall be punishable.

Section 19 of the Bill provides provisions relating to the social security. These relate to (1) Workers who are covered by social protection measures as may be prescribed by the Central or State Government. (2) The worker shall be eligible to social security protection, namely, old age, invalidity, group insurance, sickness, medical and employment injury benefits. (3) The woman worker shall be eligible for maternity benefits and childcare/davcare facility while on work. (4) The Central or the State Board through its machinery or schemes visualized for workers in all sectors will implement the social security services. (5) The State Board may frame schemes for grants to workers and loans for housing, drinking water, sanitation and other infrastructural facilities. (6) The local authorities will create and invest their resources to develop better living conditions for the workers by providing amenities like housing, safe drinking water, sanitation etc. (7) The State Board shall encourage alternate insurance for employment injury to cover employer's liability under Workmen's Compensation Act.

Section 20 of the Bill provides that work shall be permitted only in safe and healthy environment and working places. The State Government may frame appropriate rules in this regard. Section 21 of the Bill provides provision relating to working hours, holidays etc. These relate to (1) Workers shall have sufficient rest, leisure, holidays, leave and optimal working hours. (2) Maximum working hours per day shall be nine hours a day and 48 hours a week. (3) Intervals for rest of at least half an hour shall be provided after five hours of work. (4) The total number of hours of work including rest interval, shall not exceed ten and half hours in any day. (5) Worker shall be given one holiday in each week. (6) Workers shall be paid overtime wages in respect of extra hours of work put in by them on and above the hours of work.

Section 22 of the Bill deals with General provisions. These are (1) absence of any written employment contract. (2) The worker shall work diligently in the interest of the Nation. (3) Child under the age of 14 years shall not work, and shall go to school. (4) The worker shall be eligible to access the common natural resources to develop and increase his productivity through work. (5) The worker's traditional right related to work and space will be maintained. (6) Unorganised sector shall be protected from unfair labour practices. (7) No employer shall dispense with the services of an employee employed continuously for a period of not less than six months, except for a reasonable cause. The existing laws wherever they apply shall continue to apply. Nothing in this Act shall affect any better right or privilege that a worker is entitled under any other law, contract, custom, usage, award, settlement or agreement.

Section 23 (1) provides that it will be workers' duty and right to undergo skill development and on the job training, upgrading training, literacy and workers education sessions. Such programmes will be organised by the State Board and its subordinate bodies, the local government, employment providers and training institutes.[42] The State Board will devise schemes and programmes for the purpose, considering the pace of change in technology.[43] The State Board shall establish linkages with the education, training and research institutions right from local levels up to National level.[44]

The Bill, 2003 does nothing more than extending the existing laws which have never been implemented in real life till now. *Bill, 2003* does not deal with the regulation of employment of unorganised workers. There is no provision whatsoever for protection of jobs or for employment guarantee. Not only that it does not say anything about any uniform national floor-level minimum wages. It does not go a single step beyond the existing mechanism of the Minimum Wages Act. There are only provisions and promises for social security. But nothing concrete is spelt out.[45]

The draft Bill proposed by the SNCL contained nothing more than an elaborate structure of boards from the central to the panchayat level, registration of the unorganised sector workers and issue of identity cards. It contained nothing concrete to ensure job protection, minimum wages and social security for them. No responsibility was fixed on the Government to contribute for their social security.[46]

It may be observed that the Bill, 2003 need to be modified to give more protection to unorganised worker.

13. THE UNORGANISED SECTOR WORKERS' BILL, 2004

The Unorganised Sector Workers' Bill, 2004 being redrafted to promote well being to workers in unorganised sector. The Unorganised Sector Workers' Bill, 2004 is broad legislation that covers workers·scattered throughout the length and breadth of this country. The Bill focuses more on workers who work for an employer. Sadly, millions of self-employed workers get sidelined in a Bill that is specifically meant for workers belonging to the unorganised sector and to which a majority of self-employed professionals relate.

The Bill provides no social security measures for the self-employed as it does for those employed under someone. The following provision in the Bill exemplifies this clearly: "No worker shall be required to work for more than eight hours in a day with half an hour break" and "every worker shall be paid such wages within such time as may be prescribed but such wages shall in no case be less than the wages fixed under the Minimum Wages Act 1948."

These provisions do not in any way fill the gap as far as ensuring livable incomes and suitable work conditions for self-employed workers (such as hawkers and rickshaw pullers, for example) are concerned. Street vendors work more than eight hours a day, and in very difficult and many a time unfavourable conditions. Similarly, who will ensure that these workers get even a minimum wage? This is a serious loophole.[47]

For the urban poor, street vendors provide goods, including food, at low prices and rickshaws provide a cheap and accessible mode of transportation. Studies conducted by the National Alliance for Street Vendors of India show that women vendors form the lowest rungs among street vendors. Poverty and lack of jobs among male members of the family force these women to take up street hawking and vending in most cases.

Moreover, unlicensed street entrepreneurs do not have any right over the means of their livelihood. Hawkers, for example, are routinely evicted from their spaces, and their wares confiscated. It is not true that hawkers free ride on public spaces. They pay substantially to the authorities involved and suffer losses due to frequent evictions. Once caught, they have their property seized and returned to them only after the payment of a penalty. Similarly, in the case of rickshaw pullers, if caught plying without a licence, the rickshaw is confiscated, broken into pieces and auctioned.[48]

Registration System

If the government desires to know how many people are employed in a profession, it can put in place a registration system. Everyone practising a trade in the city will fill up a registration form.

The Bill's proposal to create Workers Facilitation Centres is a positive step but for the fact that it would have a predominantly bureaucratic set-up. The Bill provides that the Workers' Facilitation Centre will consist of an officer not below the rank of section officer in the government of India and such other employees as to be appointed by the appropriate government.

However, this set-up does not guarantee any internal democracy. There needs to be representations of unorganised sector workers—NGOs, hawkers' union representatives and other groups concerned need to have a voice here. Such groups not only have the trust of these workers, but they would also be more interested in ensuring that benefits and schemes reach the intended parties.

Moreover, in order to ensure that no category of worker or employer gets excluded from registration, the Workers' Facilitation Centres can take the help of ward committees/gram sabhas. Ward committee members, for example would have a better idea of the number of hawkers/vendors and rickshaw pullers in their ward. There is thus a greater probability of these street entrepreneurs not getting excluded.[49]

As of now, it is not clear how many workers' Facilitation Centres there will be at the state level and what procedure would be followed in registering workers, both self-employed and those employed under someone else, in both urban and rural areas.

As it stands today, the Bill's national coverage of workers in the informal sector (without being sensitive to self-employed professionals) gives every reason to fear that categories of self-employed and other workers of the vast informal economy, both in big and small cities and towns would get excluded. The Bill, in its entirely, does not even ensure the basic right to livelihood of unorganised sector workers. Similarly, in no part of the Bill does one see much hope for the vast majority of India's self-employed.[50]

14. UNORGANISED SECTOR WORKERS' SOCIAL SECURITY BILL, 2005

The National Commission for Enterprises in the Unorganised sector has recently drafted the Unorganised Sector Workers' Social Security Bill, 2005 proposing a universal coverage, for the unorganised workers, which is a welcome step. The draft of the Bill has come from the National Commission for Enterprises in the Unorganised Sector, set up in September 2004 "to examine the problems of the unorganised sector and suggest measures to overcome them." This Bill have been formulated after examining the Unorganised Sector Workers' Bill, 2004 prepared by the Ministry of labour and employment, government of India and the Draft of Unorganised Sector Workers' Social Security Bill prepared by the National Advisory Council.[51]

As the name suggests, the Bill attempts to provide Social Security for the unorganised workers. It provides a model by demarcating clear responsibilities of Central and State Governments. Who are covered under the scheme? According to the draft Bill it will cover all workers in the unorganised sector with a monthly income of Rs. 5,000 and below. This category includes self-employed workers (including marginal and small farmers), wage workers including agricultural labourers, and home-based workers. It also includes informal workers under the organised sector. It is estimated that around 30 crores workers are eligible under this scheme.[52]

The Bill indicates that there will be a national minimum social security for all eligible workers covering four things: (a) health insurance, (b) maternity benefits, (c) life insurance, and (d) old age pension. Every unorganised sector worker is eligible for registration. The registered worker will get a unique social security card. The existing welfare programmes will continue as before.

What are the financial implications? A National Social Security Fund will be created. The scheme will be financed from the contributions at Re. 1 a day by workers, employers (wherever identified), and the Government (that is Rs. 3 per worker a day or Rs. 1,095 a year). The Government contribution will be divided between Central Government and State Government in ratio of 3:1 respectively (75 paise per worker by the Centre and 25 paise per worker by the State Governments).

The National Commission estimated the costs of the minimum social security scheme. If all the 30 crores workers are covered, the contributions would work out to Rs. 32,850 crore. The share of the Central Government will be Rs. 17,548 crore and that of State Government Rs. 5,010 crore. This adds up to a total of Rs. 22,558 crore to be spent by Central and State Governments, equal to 0.8 percent the Gross Domestic Product in 2004-05. If we include administrative and other expenses, the government contribution may not exceed one percent of GDP. If six crore workers are covered in the first year the cost will be Rs. 4,512 crore and Rs. 22,558 crore from the fifth year. The Government can contribute to the fund in the form of grants or through tax or cess.[53]

The Bill has suggested an elaborate institutional set up for the purpose of its implementation. At the central level, there will be national social security board, supported by a general council and an executive council. There will be a secretariat with adequate professional and other staff to help the national board. At the state level there will be a state social security board, which will be supported by a state level general council and a state level executive council. Their will also be a secretariat to help the state Board. There will be a district committee for the registration of works and implementation supported by workers facilitation centres responsible for disseminating information and implementation of the Act. The delivery of social security to workers will be done either through workers' organizations or directly through any other organizations that the concerned state board decide. The workers facilitation centres will provide all the required support to the state boards in the implementation of the Act, when passed by the Parliament.[54]

Every unorganised sector worker above 18 years of age will be eligible for registration through self-declaration for registration. Each worker will get a unique social security number and an identity card which can be used any where in the country.

In short, the Bill has worked out the details of the benefits as well as the mechanism for the purpose of the implementation of the Bill.

There are however, some problems with the Bill:

First, it has not paid attention to the heterogeneous character of the unorganised sector. The unorganised workers are a highly heterogeneous group of workers. The different economic activities in the sector are at different levels in terms of technology, productivity, wages and profits. The affordability and the paying capacity of the employers as well as the needs of workers for social security will therefore be different in different activities. A uniform package will not be valid for the different categories of workers.

Secondly, financial implications have to be discussed. The commission has estimated only the likely amount of funds from the contributions. The costs of providing health insurance, and old age pension for the 30 crore workers are not clear from the Bill. The Government contribution in the first year (Rs. 4,512 crore) is not large but in the fifth year. It is closer to one percent of GDP. As the draft says, tax or cess is one option for raising resources for the Government. The insistence on State Governments' contributions may create problems for the schemes as their finances are in bad shape. Thirdly, the Bill, seems to be following the targeting approach for identifying beneficiaries. For example, the Bill says that it would cover all workers in the unorganised sector with a monthly income of Rs. 5,000 and below. This may again lead to targeting error and corruption.

Fourthly, the implementation machinery still looks

bureaucratic although decentralisation is mentioned. It is better to involve panchayati raj institutions more.

Fifthly, legislation alone is not enough. For example, health insurance for all the workers will not help if there are no doctors and health infrastructure, particularly in rural areas. Hence, spending has to increase at the grass-roots level for better delivery systems.

Sixthly, the working of the present welfare boards for workers must be examined. Kerala's experience shows that there are problems of sustainability, high costs, meagre benefits, etc. Lesson's should be learnt from these experiences.

While concluding it may be observed that this Unorganised Sector Workers' Social Security Bill, 2005 needs to be modified to support the progress (though glow) of social security movement in India. There is also a need to pay attention to the enforcement aspect of the Bill. In the final analysis, its success will largely depend on whether it address the needs and priorities of different categories of workers, the commitment and efficiency of administration, effective monitoring and workers' involvement in the implementation of the Act.

15. THE UNORGANISED SECTOR WORKERS (CONDITIONS OF WORK AND LIVELIHOOD PROMOTION) BILL, 2005

The National Commission for Enterprises in the unorganised sector has recently drafted the Unorganised Sector Workers (Conditions of Work and Livelihood Promotion) Bill 2005. This Bill has been formulated after examining the Unorganised Sector Workers' Bill, 2004, prepared by the Ministry of Labour and Employment, Government of India. The aims of the Bill was to ensure the smooth and effective implementation of social security schemes for the unorganised sector workers.

The Unorganised Sector Workers (Conditions of Work and Livelihood Promotion) Bill, 2005 seeks to address the conditions of work for those employed in the unorganised sector with a view to providing a basic minimum standard the hours of work payment of minimum wages and adherence to Bonded Labour Abolition Act and Child Labour Prohibition and Regulation Act. As for self-employed workers, the draft Bill proposes various measures for protection and promotion of livelihood. These relate to the provision of credit, right to common property and natural resources, use of public space to engage in economic activities and encourage the promotion of associations of self-employed workers.[55] The Bill also recognises some minimum entitlements of the workers such as the right to organise, non-discrimination in the payment of wages and conditions of work, safety at work place, and absence of sexual harassment.[56]

The second Bill on a conditions of workers is equally important. Some regulatory institutions are needed without ending up with Inspector Raj. Minimum wages have to be fixed keeping in view the increasing needs of the poor. The laws should be effectively implemented. Some estimates show that even if the number of days of employment are increased, the existing wages may not bring many workers above the poverty line. This is the main reason why we have so many "working poor" in the country. The poor are working but at low wages. The main issue is how to improve the wage rates for the unorganised workers.

16. THE NATIONAL RURAL EMPLOYMENT GUARANTEE ACT, 2005

Recently, the parliament has passed the historical National Rural Employment Guarantee Act, 2005, that guarantee 100 days of wage employment in a year to every rural household whose adult members are willing to do unskilled manual work. The Act will be notified in the districts identified by the Central Government starting from 2nd February, 2006 in the First phase. Initially, the Act will be in operation in 200 districts and will be extended to the whole country by 2010.

The new employment guarantee Act provides an indispensable lifelines to the millions of poor in the rural areas of the country. This social security measure, for the first time makes the right to work a fundamental right—a new radical deal for India's poor.

This landmark legislation was passed by the Lok Sabha on August 23 and the Rajya Sabha on August 24, 2005. The Bill drafted after wide consultations fulfills a major promise of the UPA's National Common Minimum Programme. The legislation has received wide support among political parties, social movements and the public at large.

Intervening in the debate on the Bill in the Rajya Sabha, Prime Minister Dr. Manmohan Singh argued for rationalizing subsidies, improving the investment climate and accelerating the pace of industrialization to maintain the economic growth of seven to eight percent to fund schemes such as Rural Employment guarantee. He described it as the most important piece of legislation" in independent India. It mark a new beginning in the efforts for social equity and justice. He hoped that in the next four or five years it would cover all rural districts.[57]

Dr. Singh said this legislation will give bargaining power to the poorest of the poor and help those belonging to the scheduled castes, scheduled tribes, landless class and women. We are offering a modest, gainful employment that will fetch Rs. 500 per month for a family. This will bring landless families in the social safety net," he said.

Replying to the debate, Rural Development Minister Shri Raghuvansh Prasad Singh assured the members that village panchayats would play a pivotal role in the implementation of the National Employment Guarantee Scheme and money would not be a constraint in accomplishing the commitments made by the UPA Government in this regard. One third of the proposed jobs would be reserved for women.

The centre has taken responsibility to provide financial assistance to the scheme and the states only had to implement it. The minimum wage as applicable in various states under the Minimum Wages Act, 1948 would apply to the programmes. However, the centre would step in to ensure a minimum rate of not less than Rs. 60 a day in states, where it was lower.[58]

The minimum wages offered for manual work in states currently varies from Rs. 25 in Nagaland to Rs. 134 in Kerala.

The Act also provides for unemployment allowance if the job, under the scheme, is not provided within a specified period. The minimum daily wage has been fixed at Rs. 60.

The UPA government has already made available about Rs. 10,000 crores for implementation of the scheme in the current financial year.[59]

Some of the salient features of the legislation are.[60]

Entitlement

- A household is entitled for 100 days of work in a year. Within the household entitlement, all adult members of a rural household have the right to demand employment.

Registration of Rural Household for Wage Employment

- A household that wants work under this Act should submit names, age, sex and addresses of its adult members to the local Gram Panchayat for registration.

Job Card to Every Registered Household

- Upon registration, a job card will be issued by the Gram Panchayat with photograph of adult members of the registered household. It will be valid for five years and will have the registration number of the household.
- A job card is a document that gives an applicant an entitlement for employment.

Application for Work

- To get employment the registered adult must submit an application on a plain paper in writing to Gram Panchayat or the Programme Officer (at block level) and get a dated receipt of the application. The application should be submitted for at least 14 days of continuous work.
- Women will get priority to the extent that one-third of persons who are given employment are women who have asked for work.

Allotment for Work

- Within 15 days from submitting the application or from the date when employment is sought, employment should be provided by the Gram Panchayat.
- Gram Panchayat will inform applicants where and when to report for work within 15 days, by means of a letter. Public notice of this will be displayed on the Gram Panchayat's Office.
- No contractor will be allowed to work under the scheme.

Payment of Unemployment Allowance

- If the eligible applicant does not get employment within 15 days of demand of work or the date from which he sought work, he shall be provided unemployment allowance. Unemployment allowance will not be less than one-fourth of the wage rate for the first thirty days during the financial year and not less than half of the wage rate for the remaining period.

Minimum Entitlement of Labourers

- The statutory minimum wage applicable to agricultural workers in the state is to be paid.
- Wages are to be paid not later than a fortnight after the date on which work was done.
- Work will be provided within 5 km of applicant residence. If employment is provided beyond 5 km radius of the applicant's residence then he is entitled to 10% additional wages towards transport and living expenses.
- At work site safe drinking water, shades for children, periods of rest and first-aid box shall be provided at every work site by the implementing agency.
- A person may be entrusted with child care responsibilities if there are more than five children

brought along on the site and that person would get paid for the work done like the other workers.

- If a workers gets injured working on the site, free medical treatment will be given by the State Government.

Creation of Durable Assets

- The focus of works is on.
- Water conservation and water harvesting.
- Drought proofing, including afforestation and tree plantation.
- Irrigation canals including micro and minor irrigation works.
- Irrigation facilities for land owners by household belonging to SC/ST or to land of beneficiaries of land reforms or that of the beneficiaries under the Indira Awas Yojana.
- Renovation of traditional water bodies, including de-silting of tanks.
- Land development.
- Flood control and protection of works, including drainage in water logged areas.
- Rural connectivity to provide all weather roads.
- Any other work, which may be notified by the Central Government in consultation with State Governments.

Implementation of the Act

- A Central Employment Guarantee Council at the Central level and State Employment Guarantee Councils at the State level in all state where the legislation is made applicable will be constitute for review, monitoring and effective implementation of the legislation in their respective areas. The Standing Committee of the District Panchayat, District Programme Coordinator, Programme Officers and Gram Panchayats have been assigned specific responsibilities in implementation of various provisions of the legislation at the Gram Panchayat, Block and District levels.

- The Gram Sabha will identify works to be taken up. The Panchayats have the principal responsibility for planning, implementing and monitoring.
- All agencies implementing NREGA will be accountable to the public for their work.
- Local Vigilance and Monitoring Committee will be set up.
- The Central Government shall establish a fund to be called 'National Employment Guarantee Fund' for the purposes of this legislation. Similarly, the State Governments may constitute State Employment Guarantee Funds. Provisions for transparency and accountability, audit, establishment of grievance and redressal mechanisms and penalty of non-compliance are also envisaged.

The key to this legislation lies in the world 'guarantee'. India abounds in schemes for the poor—all too often instruments for the state to display its munificence whenever political expediency demands it. A guarantee seeks to take this power away from the hands of the politicians and their pretenders. It makes it a right, something that people will expect and demand, something they can complain about, or in extremes, sue the government to get. It has the potential to profoundly alter the way bureaucrats treat the people they are supposed to serve.

The Employment Guarantee Scheme will be different from the many employment generation programmes. It is because they were implemented as programmes, subject to budgetary constraints and rules and regulations to suit implementing authorities. They were not statutory assured and judicially enforceable rights/entitlements of free citizens of the country. With the present Act, the State fulfils, the right of the poor to a livelihood.

However, the Guarantee Act had a limited approach. Employment must not been seen as mere manual labour. The Act must include works other than only digging and carrying mud and stones. Even the poorest in the rural areas had some skills by which they earned their livelihood. "Therefore, the Act can include the skilled work so that the employment generated is not only temporary for the 100 days but could also become of a sustained nature which could include agro-processing, on-farm processing, embroidery, weaving and printing."

The Act that has been introduced is full of ifs and buts. ... one estimate is that such a scheme would need Rs. 40,000 crores a year but the Government has not earmarked any funds, instead it seems to have passed the burden on to State Governments.

While the original promise was to include all poor rural and urban households as well as the lower middle class families, the Act has been restricted to cover only poor rural households in selected districts.

The very approach of the government is flawed. What the rural poor need is not merely a guarantee of 100 days of work in a year but uninterrupted employment throughout the year. They need creation of sources of sustainable livelihoods within their own village communities based on the concept of empowerment and not dependence on the government. As agriculture along cannot sustain the growing population in villages, it is imperative that the rural non-farm sector is strengthened.

The Act lays down that after 15 days unemployment allowance may be given in lieu of employment being unavailable. Where the economic capacity of the state prevents it, the unemployment allowance will be one fourth of the (possibly less than) minimum wage for 30 days and one-half for the rest of the year until the 100 days target is met. Who can possibly survive on less than a minimum wage or a fraction of it? Clearly the NEG Act must stick to the minimum wage as a floor guarantee. Even the promise of this unemployment allowance is illusory. If it is not paid, all that will happen is that a note will be made of it.

There is a genuine fear of large scale corruption in such programmes. But we cannot forget that these arguments are must often cited as reasons for not implementing programmes for the poor.

To conclude 93 percent of the workers in the unorganised sector do not have any social security in India. The National

Rural Employment Guarantee Act, 2005 is considered one of the important components of social security for unskilled workers. Apart from this, we need protective type social security such as old age pension, maternity benefit and health benefits. Also the conditions of workers in terms of number of hours and provisions of minimum wages need attention. In this context the two Bill prepared by the National Commission are important. It should be an important concern of public policy to ensure that a certain minimum measure of social security in the unorganised sector is ensured. This major challenge is to extend social security to 300 millions workers covering all states and all group of workers. As India has not implemented protective social security schemes on a large scale, more debate and discussions are needed for better implementation.

Notes and References

1. Report of the Second National Commission on Labour, 2002, 7.312.
2. *Ibid.*
3. Chapter-III, Section 11 to 20, The Factories Act, 1948.
4. Section 18(1), The Factories Act, 1948.
5. Section 18(3), The Factories Act, 1948.
6. Chapter-IV, Section 21 to 41, The Factories Act, 1948.
7. Section 23, The Factories Act, 1948.
8. Chapter-V, Section 42 to 48, The Factories Act, 1948.
9. Section 50(b), The Factories Act, 1948.
10. Section 10, Contract Labour (Regulation and Abolition) Act, 1970.
11. Chapter-V, Section 16 to 21, Contract Labour (Regulation and Abolition) Act, 1970.
12. Section 19, Contract Labour (Regulation and Abolition) Act, 1970.
13. Section 8, Beedi and Cigar Workers (Conditions of Employment) Act, 1966.
14. Section 9 (1), Beedi and Cigar Workers (Conditions of Employment) Act, 1966.
15. Section 10 (1), Beedi and Cigar Workers (Conditions of Employment) Act, 1966.
16. Section 24, Beedi and Cigar Workers (Conditions of Employment) Act, 1966.
17. Section 25, Beedi and Cigar Workers (Conditions of Employment) Act, 1966.
18. Section 19, Plantation Labour Act, 1951.
19. Section 25, Plantation Labour Act, 1951.
20. Section 30, Plantation Labour Act, 1951.
21. Section 32, Plantation Labour Act, 1951.
22. Section 11(1), Plantation Labour Act, 1951.
23. Section 12, Plantation Labour Act, 1951.

24. Section 8, Plantation Labour Act, 1951.
25. Section 18, Plantation Labour Act, 1951.
26. Section 15(a), Plantation Labour Act, 1951.
27. Section 5, The Dock Workers' (Regulation of Employment) Act, 1948.
28. Section 6, The Dock Workers' (Regulation of Employment) Act, 1948.
29. Section 5 A, The Dock Workers' (Regulation of Employment) Act, 1948.
30. V.V. Giri—State and Labour in India, pages 152-153, Cited by B.P. Tyagi, Labour Economics and Social Welfare, 2004, 9th edition, p. 719.
31. Section 21(5), The Mines Act, 1952.
32. Section 19(1), The Mines Act, 1952.
33. Section 28, The Mines Act, 1952.
34. Section 30, The Mines Act, 1952.
35. Section 33(1), The Mines Act, 1952.
36. Section 14, Inter-State Migrant Workmen (Regulation of Employment and Conditions of Service) Act, 1979.
37. Section 15, Inter State Migrant Workmen (Regulation of Employment and Conditions of Service) Act, 1979.
38. Section 16, Inter State Migrant Workmen (Regulation of Employment and Conditions of Service) Act, 1979.
39. Report of the Second National Commission on Labour, 2002 p. 766(i).
40. Section 13 (1), Unorganised Sector workers (Employment and Welfare) Bill, 2003.
41. Section 13 (2), Unorganised Sector workers (Employment and Welfare) Bill, 2003.
42. Section 23 (2), Unorganised Sector Workers (Employment and Welfare) Bill, 2003.
43. Section 23 (3), Unorganised Sector Workers (Employment and Welfare) Bill, 2003.
44. Section 23 (4), Unorganised Sector Workers (Employment and Welfare) Bill, 2003.
45. www.google.com, S. Kumaraswamy, Decoding the Unorganised Sector Workers' Bill, 2003.
46. http://pd.cpim.org/, People's Democracy (Weekly Organ of the Communist Party of India (Marxist), Vol. XXVII, No. 29, July 20, 2003.
47. *The Hindu*, September 18, 2005.
48. *Ibid*.
49. *Ibid*.
50. *Ibid*.
51. National Commission for Enterprises in the Unorganised Sector: Unorganised Sector Workers' Social Security Bill 2005, New Delhi.
52. *The Hindu*, September 26, 2005.
53. *Ibid*
54. Supra Notes 51.
55. *The Hindu*, Aug. 21, 2005.
56. *The Hindu*, September 26, 2005.
57. E.C. Thomas, "Job Guarantee For the Rural Poor", *Employment Newspaper*, 15-21 October, 2005.
58. *Ibid*.
59. *Ibid*.
60. *The Hindu*, January 26, 2006.

Judicial Response

"The Judiciary was to be an arm of the social revolution upholding the equality that Indians had longed for."

It is established fact that Judiciary is the third organ of the Government in any democracy. The Judiciary is the guardian of the Fundamental Rights of the people. Truly, the Supreme Court has been called upon to safeguard the rights of the people and play the role of guardian of the social revolution.[1] It is the great tribunal which has to draw the line between individual liberty and social control.[2] It is also the highest and final interpreter of the general law of the country. It is the highest Court of Appeal in civil and criminal matters.

The Judiciary in India under it policy for attainment of social justice has been very attendant to give effect the rights of unorganised labour. The role of Supreme Court in protecting poor and the weakest of the weak, unorganised labour is very appreciating. A scanning of numerous rulings reveal, the issues of juvenile justice, labour welfare, minimum wages, freedom from bondage and dignity, social security, health and children of the country. Several rights of workers in unorganised sector have been recognised by Supreme Court of India in its various judicial decisions.

In Crown Aluminium Works v. *Their Workmen*[3] the Supreme Court observed:

> "It is quite likely that in underdeveloped countries, where employment prevails on a very large scale, unorganised labour may be available on starvation wages, but the employment of labour on starvation cannot be encouraged or favoured in a modern democratic welfare State. If an employer cannot maintain his enterprise without cutting down the wages of his employees below even a bare subsistence or minimum wage, he would have no right to conduct his enterprise on such terms."

Peoples Union for Democratic Rights v. *Union of India*[4] is an epochmaking judgement of the Supreme Court which has not only made a distinct contribution to labour law but has displayed the creative attitude of judges to protect the interests of the weaker sections of the society. The Court has enlarged the contours of the fundamental right to equality, life and liberty, prohibition of traffic in human being and forced labour and prohibition of employment of child labour provided in the Constitution.

The case arose out of the denial of minimum wages to workman engaged in various Asiad Projects and non-enforcement of *The Minimum Wages Act, 1948, Equal Remuneration Act, 1976, Article 24 of the Constitution, Employment of Children Act, 1938, Contract Labour (Regulation of Employment and Conditions of Service) Act, 1979.* The Court's attention was drawn by a public-spirited organisation by means of a letter addressed to Bhagawati, J. of the Supreme Court. The Supreme Court has accepted *locus standi* of the orgnisation to file the writ petition and converted the letter into a petition and observed that when legal wrong or legal injury is caused to a person or determinate class of persons and such person or persons are unable to approach the Court for relief due to poverty, helplessness of disability or social and economic backwardness, they may be represented by any other person or organisation.

The Court has further held that employment of children below the age of 14 years in the construction work of the Asiad Project is violation of fundamental right and non-observance of the provisions of *The Equal Remuneration Act, 1976* would amount to breach of Article 14. Further, the violation of *Contract Labour (Regulation and Abolition) Act, 1970 and Inter-State Migrant Workmen (Regulation of Employment and Conditions of Service) Act, 1979* intended to ensure basic human dignity to workman is clearly in violation of Article 21. It was also held that non-payment of minimum wage to the workers engaged in construction work would amount to not only violation of *Minimum Wages Act,* but also Article 23 of the Constitution, which intends to prevent forced labour and begar. Thus, the Supreme Court has championed the cause of several person engaged in construction work of Asiad Projects and rendered justice.

In Sanjit Roy v. *State of Rajasthan,*[5] it has been held that the payment of wages lower than the minimum wages to the persons employed in Famine Relief Work is violative of Article 23. Whenever any labour or service is taken by the State from any person who is affected by drought in scarcity condition, the State cannot pay him less wage than the minimum wage on the ground that it is given them to help to meet famine situation. The State cannot take advantage of their helplessness.

In Salal Hydro Electric Project,[6] judicial intervention by means of Public Interest Litigation has yielded positive results for the benefit of the workmen employed in the Salal Hydro Electric Project. The litigation started on the basis of a news in Indian Express dated 26 August, 1982 that a large number of workmen from different States including the State of Orissa were working on he Salal Hydro Electric Project in difficult conditions and they were denied the benefits of various labour laws and were subjected to exploitation by the contractors to whom different portions of the work were entrusted by the Central Government. The People's Union for Democratic Right thereupon addressed a letter to Mr. Justice D.A. Desai enclosing a copy of the news report and requested him to treat the letter as a writ petition so that justice may be done to the poor labourers working in Salal Hydro Electric Project. The letter was treated as a writ petition and the Court directed Labour

Commissioner, Jammu to visit the site of the project and thereupon submitted a report to the Court. Pursuant to the order of the Court, the Labour Commissioner, Jammu visited the site of the project and made an interim report on October 11, 1982 followed by a final report dated October 15, 1982. The Court pointed out that since the reports made by the Labour Commissioner, Jammu disclosed that the Project was being carried out by the Government of India, the Court directed that the Union of India in the Labour Ministry as also the Chief Labour Commissioner (Central) also be added as respondents to the writ petition. Because of the directions given by the Court, the Central Government immediately with a view to secure compliance with the various directions given by the Court in an interim judgement, issued a circular to all the engineers in charge of the project who were principal employers as also to all the contractors and sub-contractors or piece wagers, directing them to make immediate compliance with the direction regarding implementation of the labour laws applicable to the workmen. The Labour Commissioner finally reported to the Court that due compliance had been made with the provisions of labour legislations, by all the parties concerned. The Court was also satisfied that the welfare amenities required to be provided under these statutes were being made to available to the workmen employed on the Salal Hydro Electric Project.

Further, in *Bandhu Mukti Morcha* v. *Union of India,*[7] the Supreme Court held that when an action is initiated in the Court through Public Interest Litigation alleging the existence of bonded labour, the Government should welcome it as it may give the Government an opportunity to examine whether bonded labour system exists and as well as to take appropriate steps to eradicate that system. This is the constitutional obligation of the Government under Article 23 which prohibits "forced labour" in any form. Article 23 has abolished the system of bonded labour but unfortunately no serious effort was made to give effect to this Article. It was only in 1976 that the Parliament enacted the *Bonded Labour System (Abolition) Act, 1976* providing for the abolition of bonded labour system with a view to preventing the economic and physical exploitation of the weaker section of the society.

In *Neeraja Chaudhary case,*[8] a writ petition was filed by a journalist in the form of a letter to Supreme Court complaining that about 135 bonded labourers within the meaning of *Bonded Labour System (Abolition) Act, 1976,* working in the stone quarries of Faridabad, had been released by the Supreme Court's order and had been brought back to M.P. with a promise of rehabilitation by the Chief Minister, but had not been rehabilitation even after six months of their release and were living in conditions to dire poverty. Giving suitable directions of the State of M.P. for implementation of the *Bonded Labour Act,* the Supreme Court observed, "It is plainest requirement of Article 21 and 23 of the Constitution that bonded labourers must be identified and released and on release, they must be suitably rehabilitated freedom from bondage without effective rehabilitation would frustrate the entire purpose of the Act, for, in that event, the freed labourers will slide back into bondage again to keep body and soul together."

The Indian judiciary to a certain extent has taken lead in securing socio-economic justice to children. In *M.C. Mehta v. State of Tamil Nadu,*[9] it has been held that the children cannot be employed in match factories which are directly connected with the manufacturing process as it is a hazardous employment within meaning of *Employment of Children Act, 1938.* They can, however, be employed in packing process but it should be done in area away from the place of manufacture to avoid exposure to accidents. Every children must be insured for a sum of Rs. 50,000 and premium to be paid by the employer as a condition of service.

In *M.C. Mehta* v. *State of Tamil Nadu,*[10] the Supreme Court while discussing statutory provisions relating to prohibition of child labour enumerated legislative enactments in force in different occupations in India clearly referred to provisions of Section 45 of the Mines Act and observed that no child shall be employed in any mine, nor shall any open cast working in which any mining operation is being carried on. After such date as the Central Government may, by notification in the Official Gazette, appoint in this behalf, no child shall be allowed to be present in any part of a mine above ground where any operation connected with or incidental to any mining operation is being carried on. After considering other legislative enactments in this regard further observed that the legislature has strongly desired prohibition of child labour. *The Child Labour (Prohibition and Regulation) Act, 1986* is, *ex facie,* a bold step.

After the commencement of *the Contract Labour (Regulation and Abolition) Act, 1970 Air India case*[11] *of 1997* is the landmark judgement given by the Apex Court. In this case the Court noted that there is no express provision under Section 10 of the CLRA Act for absorption of contract labour on abolition of the contract labour system. In the absence of such a provision the Supreme Court has played a creative role by bridging the gap left open by the legislature. Thus, in *Air India Statutory Corp.* v. *United Labour Union* case, in the majority judgement Ramaswamy, J. observed:

1. Though there is no express provision in the CLRA Act for absorption of the contract labour when engagement of contract labour stood prohibited on publication of the notification under Section 10 (1) of the Act, from that moment the principal employer cannot continue contract labour and direct relationship gets established between the workmen and the principal employer;
2. The Act did not intend to denude the contract labour of their source of livelihood and means of development throwing them out from employed; and
3. In a proper case the Court as sentinel on the *qui·vive* is required to direct the appropriate authority to submit a report and if the finding is that the workmen were engaged in violation of the provisions of the Act or were continued as contract labour despite prohibition of the contract labour under Section 10(1), the High Court has constitutional duty to enforce the law and grant them appropriate relief of absorption in the employment of the principal employer.

In a separate concurring judgement, Majmudar J. observed:

If it is held that on abolition of contract labour system, the erstwhile contract labourers are to be thrown out of that establishment lock stock and barrel, it would amount to throwing the baby out with the bath water.

He added:

> Implicit in the provision of Section 10 is the legislative intent that on abolition of contract labour system, the erstwhile contract workmen would become direct employees of the employer on whose establishment they were earlier working and were enjoying all the regulatory facilities on that very establishment under Chapter V prior to the abolition of such contract labour system. Though the legislature has expressly not mentioned the consequences of such abolition, but the very scheme and ambit of Section 10 of the Act clearly indicates the inherent legislative intent of making the erstwhile contract labourers direct employees of the employer on abolition of the intermediatory contractor.

Thus in this case it was held that the contract workers have a right to automatic absorption upon abolition.

However in *Steel Authority of India Ltd.* v. *National Union Water Front Workers and Others,*[12] a constitution bench of the Supreme Court delivered a momentous judgement having a bearing on contract labour system and ruled:

> "Neither Section 10 of the Contract Labour (Regulation and Abolition) Act nor any other provision in the Act, whether expressly or by necessary implication, provides for automatic absorption of contract labour on issuing a notification by appropriate government under Sub-Section (1) of Section 10, prohibiting employment of contract labour in any process, operation or other work in any establishment, consequently the principle employer cannot be required to order absorption of contract labour working in the concerned establishment.[13]

Thus in this case the Supreme Court has changed the law laid down in the case of *Air India Statutory Corporation* v. *United Labour Union and Others* and denied the right of contract labour to be absorbed on abolition of contract labour system, a right earlier created by another three judge bench by judicial legislation. The SAIL judgement, however, said that the *Air India case* has been wrongly decided and stated that the contract workers would have no right to automatic absorption upon abolition. But the only right available to them is they would have right to a preference in employment if permanent workers were to be employed to fill in the vacancies created by the removal of the contract workers upon abolition.[14] However, in the present scenario the Court's ruling in SAIL case in effect has succeeded in satisfying the management's desire to give them free hand to employ contract labour without imposing any liability to absorb them on abolition of the contract labour system in order to compete in the international market. Indeed, the decision is in conformity with the recommendations of the Fifth Pay Commission that in certain jobs the Government of India should also engage contract labour besides meeting some of the view points of the Finance Minister in his budget speech of the year, 2000-2001, namely, to facilitate outsourcing of activities to contract labour. In this case the Supreme Court applied the theory of hire and fire. The principles evolved in the judgement are pregnant with tremendous liability and would bring anomalous results.[15] In the era of globalization, privatization and liberalisation the effect of this judgement is far reaching. Neither can the judiciary intervene to regulate contract labour in industrial establishments, nor can a set of contract labour/workers seek protection under the Contract Act for the purpose of becoming permanent workers in the job they were engaged in on contract.

The judgement given in SAIL case was followed in *Pramod Kumar Samal and Others* v. *National Aluminium Company Ltd. and Others,*[16] in which the High Court dismissed the petition seeking a declaration of petitioners to be regular workmen as security guards, sergeants and cooks, and give direction to opposite parties to pay them remuneration equal to that paid to regular employees. The High Court observed that the contract labour was continuing in the establishment with due permission of the competent authority.

Further by virtue of a notification under Section 10 of *The Contract Labour (Regulation and Abolition) Act, 1970,* employment of contract labour in the establishment had not been prohibited.

While relying upon the decision of SAIL case Court further held that there could be no automatic absorption of contract labour on issuing notification under section 10(1) of the Act as it does not provide any such relief.

The principle of law laid down in SAIL case was followed in various recent cases also in *Cipla Ltd.* v. *Maharashtra General Kangar Union*[17] *and Food Corporation of India* v. *The Union of India and Others,*[18] while supporting the judgement of SAIL case held that workers has no right of automatic absorption on abolition of contract labour system.

The Court has taken a holistic view regarding health and labour welfare.

In *Calcutta Electric Supply Corporation* v. *Subhash Chandra Bose,*[19] Justice K. Ramaswamy in his dissenting opinion observed that health and strength of the workers is an integral facet of right to life. Thus sepeaks the Court:

To the tillers of the soil, wage earners, labourers, wood cutters, rickshaw pullars, scavengers and hut dwellers, the civil and political rights are mere cosmetic rights. Social, economic and cultural rights are their means and relevant to them to realise the basic aspirations of meaningful right to life.[20]

The juristic formulation regarding health as an investment which not only boosts productivity but also augurs good industrial relation is in the right direction. Investment in workers' health is 'like gift-edged security' as it would yield immediate return in the 'increased production'. While dwelling upon health, environment and industrial relation the learned judge proceeded to observe:

> Medical care and health facilities not only protect against sickness but also ensure stable man power for economic development. Facilities for health and medical care generate devotion and dedication to give the worker's best, physically as well as mentally, in productivity. . . . The medical facilities are, therefore, part of social security and like gift edged security, it would yield immediate return in the increased production or at any rate reduce absenteeism on ground of sickness, etc. . . . Just and favourable condition of work implies to ensure safe and healthy working conditions to the workmen. The periodical medical treatment invigorates the health of the workmen and harness their human resources.[21]

Thus he concludes:

> Prevention of occupational disabilities generates devotion and dedication to duty and enthuse the workmen to render efficient services which is a valuable asset for greater productivity to the employer and national production to the State.[22]

The copious references to health, productivity and industrial relation manifest the passion of judiciary. *In Consumer Education and Research Centre* v. *Union of India*,[23] the Apex Court was called upon to hear a writ petition by way of Public Interest Litigation praying for maintenance of compulsory health record, adoption of membrane filter as one of the measures of enviro-health protection and compulsory monetary compensation to the workmen of asbestos industry, in order to relieve the poor from handicaps, penury and distress, and to make their life liveable for greater good of society. The social justice is to be attained with substantial degree of social, economic and political equality. The Court went to the extent of declaring right to health as a part of right to livelihood and life under Article 21 read with Article 39 (e), 41, 43, 48-A of the Constitution. Thus the court observes:

> The jurisprudence of personhood or philosophy of the right to life enlarges its sweep to encompass human personality in its full blossom with invigorated health which is a wealth to the workman to earn his livelihood to sustain dignity and to live a life with dignity and equality. . . . The expression 'life' assured in Article 21 of the Constitution does not connote mere animal existence or continued drudgery through life. It has a much wider meaning which includes right to livelihood, better standard of life, by hygienic conditions in work place and liesure.[24]

The Court held that the State, be it Union or State Government or an industry, public or private is enjoined to take all such action which will promote health, strength and vigour of the workmen during period of employment and leisure and health even after retirement as basic essentials to life with health and happiness. Health of the worker enables him to enjoy the fruit of his labour. Medical facilities to protect the health of workers are, therefore, the fundamental human rights to make the life of workman meaningful and purposeful with dignity of person.

Let us turn to examine as to how the Courts have dealt with the issue, namely, whether the workers employed by the contractor in canteen may be treated as employees of the principal employer?

In *Saraspur Mills Co. Ltd.* v. *Ramanlal Chimanlal*,[25] the Supreme Court held that workers employed in a canteen even if run by a cooperative society were 'workers' as the occupier of the factory is under a mandatory obligation to maintain and run a canteen under Section 46 of *the Factories Act, 1948*.

This question was more elaborately dealt with in *M.M.R. Khan* v. *Union of India*.[26] In this case, the Supreme Court was concerned with canteen run by Railway Establishments falling under three different categories: Firstly, statutory canteens—these canteens are provided compulsorily in view of the provisions of Section 46 of the *Factories Act, 1948*. Since the Act admittedly applies to the establishments concerned and the employees working in the said establishment exceed 250. Secondly, non-statutory recognized canteens—these canteens are run in an establishment which may or may not be governed by the Act but which admittedly employ 250 or less employees and hence, it is not obligatory on the employer to maintain. However, they are set up as a staff welfare measure where the employee exceeds 100. These canteens are established with the prior approval and recognition of the employer as per the procedure contemplated under the Rules and Regulations of the Establishment; and thirdly, non-statutory and non-recognized canteens—these canteens are run at establishments under the second category but employ 100 or less than 100 employees and are established without the prior approval of or recognition of the employer.

Again in *All India Railway Institute of Employees Association* v. *Union of India*,[27] the Supreme Court dealt with this question. The Court held that the employees in the Railway Institute or Clubs were not employees of the Railway Establishment.

Parimal Chandra Raha v. *Life Insurance Corporation of India*[28] is a leading case on the subject. Here the Supreme Court ruled:

(a) Where there is a statutory obligation (e.g. under Factories Act, 1948) to provide and maintain a canteen for the use of his employees, the canteen becomes the part of the establishment and the workers employed in such canteen are the employees of the management.
(b) Where there is no statutory obligation but there is otherwise obligation on employer to provide a canteen such as part of service condition, the canteen becomes the part of the establishment and the workers employed in such canteen are the employees of the management.
(c) Where there is no obligation to provide a canteen but there is an obligation to provide facilities to run canteen, the canteen does not become a part of the establishment.

However, in *Indian Petrochemicals Corporation Ltd. and another v. Shramic Sena and Others,*[29] a new gloss was given to this decision by stating that the presumption arising under the *Factories Act* in relation to such workers is available for the purpose of he Act and no further. The Supreme Court held that the *Factories Act, 1948* does not govern the rights of employee with respect to (i) recruitment (ii) seniority (iii) promotion (iv) retirement benefits, etc. These are governed by other statutes, rules, contracts or policies. Therefore, employees of the statutory canteen cannot *ipso facto* become the employees of the establishment for all purpose. The Court added that (i) It should be borne in mind that the initial appointments of these workmen are not in accordance with the rules governing appointments; (ii) Rules governing establishments; (iii) Rules governing policy of recruitment of the management; (iv) The aforesaid recruitments could also be in contravention of the various statutory orders including reservation policy; (v) Further as an instrumentality of the State has an obligation to conform to the requirements of Articles 14 and 16 of the Constitution; (ii) In spite of the same, the services of the workmen are being regularized by the Supreme Court not as a matter of right of workmen but with a view to eradicate unfair labour practices and bring equity to undo social injustice.

The Supreme Court again in *Indian Overseas Bank* v. *I.O.B Staff Canteen Workers' Union and another,*[30] while considering the effect of *Parimal Chandra Raha and Others* v. *L.I.C. of India and Others and Indian Peterochemical Corp. Ltd. and another v. Shramic Sena and Others* ruled that the workers of a particular canteen statutorily obliged to be run a canteen render to more than to deem them to be workers for limited purpose of the Factories Act and not for all purposes and in cases where it is a non-statutory recognized canteen the Court should find out whether the obligation to run was implicit or explicit on the facts proved in that case and the ordinary test of control, supervision and the nature of facilities provided were taken note of to find out whether the employees therein are those of the main establishment."

In *Barat Fritz Werner Limited* v. *State of Karnataka,*[31] the Supreme Court ruled that the workers working in canteens even if employed through the contractor have to be treated as "workers" and no restricted meaning can be given even where the *Factories Act, 1948* is not applicable to an establishment but canteen facility is provided as a condition of service.

In *Hari Shankar Sharma and Ors.* v. *Artificial Limbs Manufacturing Corporation and Ors,*[32] the Supreme Court held that the employees of a statutory set up, or of any other facility, provided, by the establishment in discharge of statutory mandate need not necessarily be employees of the establishment as Section 46 of *Factories Act* leaves it to the discretion of establishment to resort to direct employment or to employ a contractor and their status depends upon the manner of discharge of statutory obligations. There it was further held that the condition in the agreement between the contractor and the establishment that the new contractor should retain the employees who had served under the earlier contractors would not necessarily mean that such employees were employees of the establishment.

In *Mishra Dhattu Nigam Ltd.* v. *M. Venkataiah and Ors.,*[33] the Supreme Court held since the management was required by the *Factories Act,* to provide canteen facilities, the workers engaged through the contractors were the employees of the principal employer, and the canteen workers engaged through the contractors were entitled to regularisation of their services.

In *Gopalakrishnan and Others v. Cochin Port Trust,*[34] the only question that arose in this petition was whether petitioners who were employees of the canteen established by Cochin Port Trust, were entitled in regularisation in the service of the Port Trust. The High Court held they were so entitleld and allowed the petition. It observed the canteen in question was a statutory canteen established under Section 46 of the *Factories Act, 1948.* The Port Trust was having over all control, including, financial, over the functioning of the canteen.

The petitioners were therefore held entitled to be treated as employees of the Port Trust subject to their eligibility at time of appointment as to age limit, health standard, educational qualification etc.

In Haldia Refinery Canteen Employees Union and Another v. Indian Oil Corporation Ltd. and others,[35] settling a lingering debate, the Supreme Court has ruled that even if management of an organisation exercises control over the types of workers to be engaged in its canteen run by a contractor, they do not become employees of the office concerned.[36]

The ruling was given by a bench comprising Justice Ashok Bhan and Justice A.K. Mathur, while dismissing an appeal filed by Haldia Refinery Canteen Employees Union Challenging a Calcutta High Court Judgement.

In this case the appellants are working in the statutory canteen run by the respondent through contractor in its factory at Haldia, District Midnapore, West Bengal. Respondent was treating the appellant as the employees of the contractor. Aggrieved against this the appellant filed the writ applications in the High Court.

Appellant-Employees Union, despite initial success before single judge, could not retain it when the respondent cooperation took the matter up in appeal before a Division Bench. It held the appellants were not entitled to regularisation as the employees of the respondent, since they were employees of the contractor who ran the canteen, albeit statutory, in the factory of respondent. Aggrieved against the aforesaid judgement of the Division Bench, the present appeal has been filed in Supreme Court by appellant—Employee Union.

The Supreme Court, after going through the conditions of the contract, observed the control that the respondent exercised over the contractor, was only to ensure that the canteen was run in efficient manner. It did not mean the canteen employees (by virtue of such control) became the employment of the management.

Workmen in a statutory canteen such as the appellants, became workers of the establishment for the purpose of the Factories Act, 1948 only and not for any other purpose, the Supreme Court pointed out.

The Supreme Court referred also to certain facts which rendered the claim of the appellants not tenable. First, the management was not reimbursing to the contractor the wages of the workmen. Second, two settlements had been made between the contractor and the canteen workmen. The respondent was not a party to either of them. So the appeal dismissed.

This ruling assumes significance since the apex court had, in its earlier judgements held that the workers in a canteen attached to an office would be treated as employees of that office if the management exercised control over the selection of the canteen workers and payment of their salaries, even if they were being engaged by a contractor.

An analysis of the various cases reveals that the Judiciary have done a good job for the protection of the rights of unorganised labour. *The Crown Aluminium Works, Peoples Union for Democratic Rights, Sanjit Roy, Salal Hydroelectric Project, Bandhu Mukti Morcha, Neeraja Chaudhary and two Cases of M.C. Mehta* are the landmark decisions of the Supreme Court wherein several rights of the individual especially the workers in the unorganised sector have been upheld and safeguarded.

In the present scenario the judgement of *Steel Authority of India* is not appropriate as it left the workers in void while providing the employers a free hand to appoint more contract labourers without any responsibility to absorb them on abolition. The principles evolved in the judgement are pregnant with tremendous liability and would bring anomalous results. In the era of globalization, privatization and liberalisation the effect of this judgement is far reaching. Neither can the judiciary intervene to regulate contract labour in industrial establishments, nor can a set of contract labour/workers seek protection under the Contract Act for the purpose of becoming permanent workers in the job they were engaged in on contract.

Hence, the need of the hour is to review the judgement of *Steel Authority of India.*

Coming to canteen employees the Supreme Court settling a lingering debate, has ruled in *Haldia Refinery Canteen Employees Union and another* v. *Indian Oil Corporation Ltd. and others* case that even if management of an organisation exercises control over the types of workers to be engaged in its canteen run by a contractor, they do not become employees of the office concerned.

The Supreme Court, after going through the conditions of the contract, observed the control that the respondent exercised over the contractor, was only to ensure that the canteen was run in efficient manner. It did not mean the canteen employees (by virtue of such control) became the employment of the management.

Workmen in a statutory canteen such as the appellants, became workers of the establishment for the purpose of the Factories Act, 1948 only and not for any other purpose, the Supreme Court pointed out.

This ruling assumes significance since the apex court had, in its earlier judgements held that the workers in a canteen attached to an office would be treated as employees of that office if the management exercised control over the selection of the canteen workers and payment of their salaries, even if they were engaged by a contractor.

Notes and References

1. G. Austin—The Indian Constitution Cornerstone of Nation, p. 169, Cited by J.N. Pandey, Constitutional Law of India, 38th edition, 2002, p. 421.
2. Sri Alladi Krishnaswamy Aiyer, Member of Drafting Committee, Cited by J.N. Pandey, Constitutional Law of India, 38th edition, 2002, p. 421.
3. (1958), 1.L.L.J. 1.
4. (1982), 2.L.L.J. 454
5. AIR 1983 S.C. 1155.
6. Salal Hydro Electric Project *v.* State of J&K (1983) 2SCC 181.
7. A.I.R. 1984 S.C. 802.
8. Neeraja Chaudhary *v.* State of M.P., A.I.R. 1984 SC 1099.
9. AIR 1991 SC 417.
10. 1997 SCC (L and S) 49.

11. Air India Statutory Corp. *v.* United Labour Union, 1997 LLR 288.
12. 2001, 111 LLR 349.
13. *Ibid.*
14. Sanjay Singhvi: "A Raw deal for Contract Labour", Labour file Dec. 2001.
15. Suresh C. Srivastava, "Impact of the Supreme Court decision on Contract Labour", *Journal of the Indian Law Institute,* Vol. 43:4, 2001.
16. 2002 III LLJ, Orri p. 657.
17. 2001 LLR 305.
18. 2003 Lab. IC p. 166.
19. A.I.R. (1992) S.C. 573.
20. *Ibid.,* at 585.
21. *Ibid.*
22. *Ibid.*
23. A.I.R. (1995) S.C. 922.
24. *Ibid.,* at 8-39.
25. (1973) 3 SCR 967.
26. 1990 (Supp) SSC 191.
27. (1991) 2 Lab LJ 265.
28. 1995 Supp (2) SCC 611.
29. 1999 (6) SCC 439.
30. 2000 (4) SCC 245.
31. 2001 LLR 285.
32. 2002(1) SCC 387.
33. 2003-III LLJ 897.
34. 2004-II-LLJ.
35. 2005 II LL.J.
36. *Hindustan Times,* May 4, 2005.

Conclusion and Suggestions

The foregoing study brings the conclusion that unorganised sector could not be defined and identified solely on the basis of the nature of work of the workers or on the basis of the number of employees in the undertaking and also not on the level of organisation. The unorganised sector is too vast to remain within the confines of a conceptual definition. Hence many efforts have been made to identify the characteristics of employments or undertakings in the sector. But none of the characteristics can be termed as crucial in defining the sector. However, it can be said there are some special features such as low wages and low earnings, high percentage of employment of women, employment of family labour, child labour, migrant labour, piece-rate payments, home-based work or contractual work, seasonal or intermittent employment, lack of organisation into trade unions, casual and multiple jobs, existence of debt bondage, existence of cooperatives of self-employed workers, dependence on others for supply of raw material, less access to capital, existence of health hazards are often used to define and identify the unorganised sector.

The unorganised sector workers have not acquired a high profile, tasted the benefits that can be gained from organisation, or deprived the advantageous flowing from high visibility. They are extremely poor, illiterate and exploited in many ways. They work for long hours and do variety of work and sometimes get few hours of undisturbed sleep. They are exposed to all the vagaries of climate and winter, such as scorching sun, heavy rain and chilly winter while at work. Workers are exposed to serious health hazards which affect their longevity.

Thus, Governments have paid due attention towards miserable living conditions of unorganised sector workers. In 1947, the *International Labour Organisation* laid down the framework of labour welfare and also spelt out the services and amenities which should be included in this framework. With the clear guidance from this highest Organisation of labour in the world, attention also paid in India towards the welfare of unorganised labour. The labour policy set out in the *Five-Year Plans* since independence was based on the belief that the basic need of workers for food, clothing and shelter must be satisfied. An important aspect of labour policy outlined in the *Seventh Plan (1985-90)* relates to the formulation of an appropriate wage policy, and provisions for the welfare and working and living conditions of unorganised labour not only in the rural sector but also in urban areas. The *Eighth Plan* (1992-1997) said that improvement in the quality of labour, productivity, skills and working conditions and provision of welfare and social security measures, especially of those working in unorganised sector was crucial for enhancement of the status of labour. The Plan laid emphasis on the enforcement of labour laws especially laws relating to unorganised labour and women and child labour. However, it has to be admitted that the *Five-Year Plans* did not formulate an integrated and comprehensive scheme of social security for unorganised labour.

The Framers of Indian Constitution also paid due attention to the amelioration of the working class of the country. The Indian Constitution has made a specific mention of the duties that the State owes to the labour, to their economic upliftment and social regeneration. Apart from constitutional mandate, social security for all considered as a basic Human Right Under the *Universal Declaration of Human Rights*. Every member nation of U.N.O. must strive to further and promote this basic right. Many schemes and policies have been evolved both at central and state level to provide social security to the workers in the unorganised sector. Inspite of these provisions, schemes and policies, the result is not so satisfactory because of non-implementation of the schemes properly. Even new social security scheme is launched by Prime Minister Atal Bihari Vajpayee on Feb. 22, 2004. Beside this in November 14, 2004 National Food for Work Programme has been launched. In the year 2005, Rajiv Gandhi Shramik Kalyan Yojana, National Rural Health Mission, Bhoomi Sena Scheme, Tamil Nadu Chief Minister's Farmers Security Scheme has been launched. If these schemes are not properly implemented the same with the other schemes.

There are many labour legislation. All of them do not cover workers engaged in unorganised sector. Some are applicable. But none of the laws that form the base of social security system covers the whole unorganised sector. There are laws that apply wholly or partly to this sector. The *Factories Act, 1948* is applicable to the workers in the unorganised sector where there is an identifiable employer-employee relationship. Its provisions do not apply to vass masses of workers in the unorganised sector. The *Minimum Wages Act, 1948* is the most important law enacted for the benefit of unorganised labour. The Act is meant to ensure that the market forces and the law of demand and supply are not allowed to determine the wages of workers covered by this law. 60% of the workforce in unorganised sector is self-employed or home-based and thus remain outside the purview of the *Minimum Wages Act. The Contract Labour (Regulation and Abolition) Act, 1970* regulates the employment of contract labour in certain establishments and provides for its abolition in certain circumstances. This Act is meant for unorganised labour. But its scope is very limited. It is not applicable to a contractor who employs less than 20 workers which leads to manipulations by employers and contractors.

Besides this, there are a long list of labour legislations, i.e. *Beedi and Cigar Workers (Conditions of Employment) Act, 1966, Plantation Labour Act, 1951, Building and Other Construction Workers' (Regulation of Employment and Conditions of Service) Act, 1996, Dock Workers' (Regulation of Employment) Act, 1948,*

Payment of Wages Act, 1936, the Mines Act, 1952, Workmen's Compensation Act, 1923, Inter-State Migrant Workmen (Regulation of Employment and Conditions of Service) Act, 1979, under which various categories of unorganised sector are covered.

The scope of these Act is very limited. It looks anomalous that unorganised workers can receive the limited benefits of the existing labour laws only if they happen to work for employers, in other words, if there is an employer-employee relationship. None of these labour laws can provide protection to the vast majority of unorganised workers who are self-employed or home-based or to other workers who are employed in enterprises where the number of employees does not reach the threshold prescribed by the Acts. Hence these laws have proved inadequate to ensure work security and social security to the workers in the unorganised sector or to safeguard their constitutional rights.

In order to ensure, under an umbrella legislation, economic and social security to all unorganised sector workers and to mould them into a productive and secure workforce, an Act on unorganised sector workers employment and welfare is needed.

The Unorganised Sector Workers (Employment and Welfare) Bill, 2003 is the logical outcome of the Second National Labour Commission's recommendations. An Act to consolidate and amend the laws relating to the regulation of employment and welfare of workers in the unorganised sector in India and to provide protection and social security to these workers.

The Bill, 2003 provides provisions relating to minimum wages allowances, social security, health and safety, holidays, education, training and skill development. It also provides provisions relating to constitution of Boards, functions of Central Board, State Board, Employment based Boards, District Boards and State Board in relation to self-employed workers. Provisions relating to registers and records, grievance redressal, framing of rules and schemes also provided in the Bill.

The Bill, 2003 does nothing more than extending the existing laws which have never been implemented in real life till now. It does not deal with the regulation of employment of unorganised workers. There is no provision whatsoever for protection of jobs or for employment guarantee. Not only that it does not say anything about any uniform national floor-level minimum wages. There are only provisions and promises for social security. But nothing concrete is spelt out.

The Unorganised Sector Workers' Bill, 2004 is broad legislation that covers workers scattered throughout the length and breadth of this country. Sadly, millions of self-employed workers get sidelined in a Bill that is specifically meant for workers belonging to the unorganised sector and to which a majority of self-employed professionals relate.

The Unorganised Sector Workers' Social Security Bill, 2005 attempts to provide social security for the unorganised workers. It provides a model by demarcating clear responsibilities of Central and State Governments. It will cover all workers in the unorganised sector with a monthly income of Rs. 5,000 and below. It is estimated that around 30 crores workers are eligible under the scheme.

But, unfortunately the Bill has not paid attention to the heterogeneous character of unorganised sector. It may be observed that this Unorganised Sector Workers' Social Security Bill, 2005 needs to be modified to support the progress (though slow) of social security movement in India. Its success will largely depend on whether it address the needs and priorities of different categories of workers, the commitment and efficiency of administration, effective monitoring and workers' involvement in the implementation of the Act.

The Unorganised Sector Workers (Conditions of Work and Livelihood Promotion) Bill, 2005 deals with conditions of work and livelihood promotion for those employed in the unorganised sector. The aims of the Bill was to ensure the smooth and effective implementation of social security schemes for the unorganised sector workers. This Bill is equally important. Some regulatory institutions are needed without ending up with Inspector Raj. Minimum Wages have to be fixed keeping in view the increasing needs of the poor.

The National Rural Employment Guarantee Act, 2005 guarantee 100 days of wage employment in a year to every rural household whose adult member are willing to do unskilled manual work. The Employment Guarantee Scheme is considered one of the important components of social security for unskilled workers. However, the Guarantee Act had a limited approach. Employment must not been seem as mere manual labour. The Act must include works other than only digging and carrying mud and stones. The very approach of the government is flawed what the rural poor need is not merely a guarantee of 100 days of work in a year but uninterrupted employment throughout the year. The Act, will in all livelihood remain on paper without scope for implementation. Its success will largely depend on its implementation.

The judiciary anxiety and anguish towards the problem of workers engaged in unorganised sector was well amplified in various judgements and the judiciary made earnest efforts to secure the rights and protect the interests of unorganised sector workers.

Peoples Union for Democratic Rights[1] case is an epochmaking judgement of the Supreme Court which has not only made a distinct contribution to labour laws but has displayed the creative attitude of judges to protect the interests of the weaker section of the society. The Court has enlarged the contours of the fundamental right to equality, life and liberty, prohibition of traffic in human being and forced labour and prohibition of employment of child provided in the Constitution.

The *Crown Aluminium Works,*[2] *Sanjit Roy,*[3] *Salal Hydro Electric Project,*[4] *Bandhua Mukti Morcha,*[5] *Neeraja Chaudhary,*[6] two cases of *M.C. Mehta*[7] and *Air India Statutory Corporation*[8] are the landmark decisions of the Supreme Court where in several rights of the individual especially the workers engaged in the unorganised sector have been upheld and safeguarded.

Coming to canteen employees the Supreme Court settling a lingering debate, has ruled in *Haldia Refinery Canteen Employees Union and another* v. *Indian Oil Corporation Ltd. and others*[9] case that even if management of an organisation exercises control over the types of workers to be engaged in its canteen run by a contractor, they do not become employees of the office concerned.

The Supreme Court, after going through the conditions of the contract, observed the control that the respondent exercised over the contractor, was only to ensure that the canteen was run in efficient manner. It did not mean the canteen employees (by virtue of such control) became the employment of the management.

Workmen in a statutory canteen such as the appellants, became workers of the establishment for the purpose of the Factories Act, 1948 only and not for any other purpose, the Supreme Court pointed out.

This ruling assumes significance since the apex court had, in its earlier judgements held that the workers in a canteen attached to an office would be treated as employees of that office if the management exercised control over the selection of the canteen workers and payment of their salaries, even if they were engaged by a contractor.

In the present scenario the judgement of *Steel Authority of India*[10] is not appropriate as it left the workers in void while providing the employers a free hand to appoint more contract labourers without any responsibility to absorb them on abolition. This judgement demolished what little protection the law had so far afforded contract labour. The principles evolved in the judgement are pregnant with tremendous liability and would bring anomalous results. In the era of globalization, privatization and liberalisation the effect of this judgement is far reaching. Neither can the judiciary intervene to regulate contract labour in industrial establishments, nor can a set of contract labour/workers seek protection under *the Contract Act* for the purpose of becoming permanent workers in the job they were engaged in on contract. Hence it is submitted that Supreme Court would review the judgement of *Steel Authority of India*.

However, this would not be correct to say that nothing has been done to provide effective social protection to workers engaged in unorganised sector. Legislative prescriptions and judicial responses have tried to give effect the rights of unorganised sector workers and many positive steps in right direction are taken, but unfortunately, the result is not so satisfactory as we thought, it is only because of :

(a) Lack of adequate machinery to create awareness of the statutory benefits among unorganised sector workers;
(b) Ineffective scale of punished provided by the statute;
(c) Lack of vigour and motivation for enforcement among the administrative authorities;
(d) The workers engaged in unorganised sector are not conscious of the laws and acquire the strength to ensure that laws are brought into force;

(e) Lack of permanent or stable linkage between employer and employee that precludes schemes based on employer's contribution;

(f) There are not effective means to implement, monitor and provide quick redress.

Hence, in the context of Indian conditions with the prevalence of such constraining factors, the protection of interests of unorganised sector workers is a difficult task, but not impossible. The need of hour is to create awareness among the workers engaged in unorganised sector about their rights and proper implementation of the laws, schemes and policies.

SUGGESTIONS

The present study prompts us to put forth some suggestions as under:

1. Understanding of the problems of different categories of unorganised sector is essential for formulation of suitable ameliorative measures for welfare. First hand detailed surveys of these categories should be undertaken from time to time to study their problems and conditions of work.
2. To ensure better and more effective enforcement of the laws a strong political will coupled with active co-operation from the public is a must. Social workers and voluntary Organisation should be persuaded to associate themselves with the law enforcement process.
3. The Government must approach the issues relating to unorganised sector not merely from a welfare point of view but from the angle of regulation of employment and to guarantee a minimum earning capacity for the workers.
4. Employees State Insurance and Provident Fund Scheme should be extended to the unorganised sector as well. The social security schemes must address, health, maternity benefit, disability and old age income security concerns.
5. As the unogranised sector comprises 92 per cent of our working age population, both the Central and State

Governments must contribute a proportion of their revenue and also levy a cess from the employers, for extending the welfare and social security benefits to these workers.

6. To make schemes effective, governmental and non-governmental organisations must be encouraged. Further more and more social assistance programmes be evolved because in case of social insurance schemes the workers in the unorganised sector are unable to contribute regularly due to uncertainty of income etc. But at the same time there must be a proper control and check to prevent misuse of the social assistance programmes.
7. The problem of workers' welfare is of such a great magnitude that no single agency alone can tackle it successfully. Therefore the welfare work should be considered a joint responsibility of the Central and State Governments, employers and trade unions. They should all work in harmony to raise the standard of living of the workers.
8. The central trade unions and the employer's organisations must be equally represented on the tripartite bodies relating to the unorganised sector. Also, their participation must be ensured in the process of formulation and preparation of schemes for the benefit of unorganised workers.
9. The judicial pronouncement on the question of absorption of contract labour as given in *Steel Authority of India's case* that the workers would have no right to automatic absorption upon abolition seems left them in void. The Court's ruling in effect, has succeeded in satisfying the management's desire to give, them free hand to employ more contract labours. The judgement given by the Court in *Air India Statutory Corporation* case provides the relief to the workers by giving them the right of automatic absorption on the abolition of contract labour. It seems that both the cases have failed to make a balance to satisfy the needs of the employer and workers and while providing any relief to any party created hardship for the others. Hence it is

submitted that there must be a clear cut policy of the Government on the matter of automatic absorption of contract labour.

10. The decision of Supreme Court in *Steel Authority of India case* on giving preference to contract labour in employment when vacancy of regular workmen arises creates a conflict between Section 25 H of the Industrial Disputes Act, 1947 and the judicial legislation created by the Court in this case. To resolve this dispute it is submitted that a mechanism must be created through which only those workers are absorbed on abolition that are efficient workers.
11. Some cover for underemployment and loss of jobs should be introduced, as the sector has many occupations of a seasonal nature, incidence of loss of jobs etc. In Kerala, group insurance schemes have been introduced for fish-workers. Such schemes should be formulated with such improvements.
12. The agricultural workers are becoming a dynamic assertive and independent class of rural India and they are the motive force of revolutionary democracy. Therefore, the agricultural workers must not in general be clubbed with the unorganised sector. Rather, a separate national level legislation must be enacted for the benefit of agricultural workers, covering workers in farming, horticulture, sericulture and other like sectors.

Notes and References

1. Peoples Union for Democratic Rights v. Union of India, (1982), 2 L.L.J. 454.
2. Crown Auminium Works v. Their Workmen, (1958), 1.L.L.J.1.
3. Sanjit Roy *v.* State of Rajasthan, AIR 1983 S.C. 1155.
4. Salal Hydro Electric Project v. State of J and K. (1983) SCC 181.
5. Bandhua Mukti Morcha v. Union of India, A.I.R. 1984 S.C. 802.
6. Neeraja Chaudhary v. State of M.P., AIR 1984 SC 1099.
7. M.C. Mehta v. State of Tamil Nadu, AIR 1991 SC 417.
8. Air India Statutory Corporation v. United Labour Union, 1997 LLR 288.
9. Haldia Refinery Canteen Employees Union and another v. Indian Oil Corporation Ltd. and Others 2005-II LLJ.
10. Steel Authority of India v. National Union Water Front Workers and Others, 2001 LLR 961.

Table of Cases

Air India Statutory Corporation *v.* United Labour Union, 1997 LLR 288.

All India Railway Institute of Employees Association *v.* Union of India (1991) 2 Lab. LJ 265.

Bandhua Mukti Morcha *v.* Union of India, A.I.R. 1984 S.C. 802.

Barat Fritz Werner Limited *v.* State of Karnataka, 2001 LLR 285.

Calcutta Electric Supply Corporation *v.* Subhash Chandra Bose, AIR (1992) S.C. 573.

Cipla Ltd. *v.* Maharashtra General Kamgar Union, 2001 LLR 305.

Consumer Education and Research Centre *v.* Union of India, A.I.R. (1995) S.C. 922.

Crown Aluminium Works *v.* Their Workmen, (1958) 1 L.L.J. 1.

Food Corporation of India *v.* The Union of India and Others, 2003 Lab IC p. 166.

Gopalkrishnan and Others *v.* Cochin Port Trust, 2004-II-LLJ.

Haldia Refinery Canteen Employees Union and another *v.* Indian Oil Corporation Ltd. and Others, 2005-II-LLJ.

Hari Shankar Sharma and Others *v.* Artificial Limbs Manufacturing Corporation and Others, 2002 (1) SCC 387.

Indian Petrochemicals Corporation Ltd. and another *v.* Shramic Sena and Others, 1999 (6) SCC 439.

Indian Overseas Bank *v.* I.O.B. Staff Canteen Workers' Union and another, 2000 (4) SCC 245.

M.C. Mehta *v.* State of Tamil Nadu, AIR 1991 SC 417.

M.C. Mehta *v.* State of Tamil Nadu, 1997 SCC (L and S) 49.

M.M.R. Khan *v.* Union of India, 1990 (supp) SCC 191.

Mishra Dhattu Nigam Ltd. *v.* M. Venkataiah and Ors., 2003-III LLJ 897.

National Federation by Rly. Porters, Vendors and Bearers *v.* Union of India, 1995 SCC (L and S) 1119.

Neeraja Chaudhary *v.* State of M.P., AIR 1984 SC 1099.

Parimal Chandra Raha *v.* Life Insurance Corporation of India, 1995 supp (2) SCC 611.

Peoples Union for Democratic Rights *v.* Union of India, (1982) 2 L.L.J. 454.

Pramod Kumar Samal and Others *v.* National Aluminium Company Ltd. and Others, 2002 111 LLJ Orri p. 657.

Salal Hydro Electric Project *v.* State of J and K (1983) 2 SCC 181.

Sanjit Roy *v.* State of Rajasthan, AIR 1983 S.C. 1155.

Saraspur Mills Co. Ltd. *v.* Ramanlal Chimanlal, (1973) 3 SCR 967.

Steel Authority of India Ltd. *v.* National Union Water Front Workers and Others, 2001, 111 LLR 349.

T.N. Electricity Employees and Contract Labour Union *v.* T.N. Electricity Board, 1995 SCC (L and S) 1130.

Bibliography

Books

Baxi, U., 'Law and Poverty—Critical Essay', (1988), N.M. Tripathi Private Limited.

De, D.J., 'Interpretation and Enforcement of Fundamental Rights', (2000), Eastern Law House Pvt. Ltd., Calcutta.

Giri, V.V., 'Labour Problems in Indian Industry', (1958), Asia Publishing House, Bombay.

Goswami, V.G., 'Labour and Industrial Laws', (7th edition, 1999), Central Law Agency, Allahabad-2.

Hasan, N., 'The Social Security System of India', (Ist edition, 1972), S. Chand and Co. (Pvt.). Ltd., New Delhi-55.

Jain, M.P., 'Indian Constitutional Law', (4th edition, 1994), Smt. Rampyari Wadhwa, Agra.

Misra, S.N., 'Labour and Industrial Laws', (19th edition, 2003), Central Law Publications, Allahabad.

Pandey, J.N., 'Constitutional Law of India', (38th edition, 2002), Central Law Agency, Allahabad-2.

Pai, G.B., 'Labour Law in India', Vols. 1 and 2, (2001), Butterworths India, New Delhi.

Pillai, K.M., 'Labour and Industrial Law', (19th edition, 2003), Allahabad Law Agency Law Publishers, Faridabad (Haryana).

Puri, S.K., 'Labour and Industrial Law', (8th edition, 2002), Allahabad Law Agency, Faridabad (Haryana).

Saxena, R.C., 'Labour Problem and Social Welfare', (1981), K. Nath and Co. Educational Publishers and Printers, Meerut.

Shukla, V.N., 'Constitution of India', (9th edition, 1996), Eastern Book Company, Lucknow.

Srivastava, S.C., 'Treaties on Social Security and Labour Laws', (1985), Eastern Book Co., Lucknow.

Tyagi, B.P., 'Labour Economics and Social Welfare', (9th edition, 2004), Jai Prakash Nath and Co., Meerut.

Yadav, L.B., 'Readings in Social and Labour Welfare', Vol. 3 (Ist edition, 2000), Anmol Publications Pvt. Ltd.

Zaheeruddin, 'Case and Material on Labour Laws', (2003).

Zaheeruddin, 'Labour Welfare Laws and Employment Conditions in India', (1985), Deep and Deep Publications, New Delhi.

Articles

Akhtar, Saleem, M. Zafar Mahfooz Nomani, Haris Umar, 'Legislative and Institutional Framework for Elimination of Child Labour: An Analysis', *Aligarh Law Journal*, Vol. XII, (1997).

Dev, S. Mahendra, 'Social Security for Indian Workers: Performance and Issues', *The Indian Journal of Labour Economics*, Vol. 39, No. 4, (1996).

Dicthrich, Gabriele, 'Construction Workers at Cross Roads', *Economic and Political Weekly*, September, (1992).

Nadagoudar, Suresh V., 'Social Security for Workers in the Unorganised Sector', *Cochin University Law Review*, Vol. XXVI, March and June, No. 1 and 2, (2002).

Nomani, Md. Zafar Mahfooz, 'Health Environment and Industrial Relation: Emerging Judicial Trends in India', *The Academy Law Review*, Vol. 20 : 1 and 2, (1996).

Rao, V. Mohan, "Quality Healthcare for Rural Poor", *Employment Newspaper*, June 11-17 (2005).

Sasikumar, S.K., R.K.A. Subrahmanya, 'Social Security for the Unorganised Workers', *The Indian Journal of Labour Economics*, Vol. 39, No. 4, (1996).

Sen, Arup Kumar, 'Mode of Labour Control in Colonial India', *Economic and Political Weekly*, September 21, (2002).

Singhvi, Sanjay, 'A Raw Deal for Contract Labour', *Labour File* Dec. (2001).

Srivastava, Suresh C., 'Impact of the Supreme Court Decision in Contract Labour (Steel Authority of India Ltd. *v.* National

Union Water Front)', *Journal of the Indian Law Institute*, Vol. 43 : 4, (2001).

Thomas, E.C., "Job Guarantee for the Rural Poor", *Employment Newspaper*, October 15-21 (2005).

Reports Debates and Plans

Constitutive Assembly Debates 19th Nov. 1948.

Five Year Plans: First (1951-56), Second (1956-61), Third (1961-62 to 1965-66), Fourth (1967-74), Fifth (1974-79), Sixth (1980-85), Seventh (1985-90), Eighth (1992-97).

Report of the First National Commission on Labour, 1969.

Report of the Second National Commission on Labour, Vol. 1 and 2, 2002.

Report of the Labour Investigation Committee, 1946.

Report of the Labour Investigation Committee, 1964.

Report of the National Commission on Rural Labour, 1991.

Report of the Royal Commission on Labour in India, 1931.

Report of the Royal Commission on Labour in India, 1969.

Report of Study Group on Social Security, 1957.

Report of the Committee on Labour Welfare, 1969.

Report of Rege Committee on Labour, 1944.

Report of the National Commission on Self-Employed Women and Women in the Informal Sector (Shramshakti), 1988.

The Beveridge Report on Social Insurance and Allied Services, 1942.

The Annual Report of the Ministry of Labour, 1999-2000.

Dictionaries

Chamber 21st Century Dictionary.

Chamber 29 Century Dictionary.

Osborn's Concise Law Dictionary.

P. Ramanatha Aiyar Concise Law Dictionary.

The Concise Oxford Dictionary.

Webstar Third New International Dictionary.

News Papers

Employment Newspaper, April 30 – May 6, 2005.

Employment Newspaper, June 11-17, 2005.

Employment Newspaper, October 15-21, 2005.

The Hindustan Times, February 23, 2004.

The Hindu, January 18, 2004.
The Hindu, February 23, 2004.
The Hindustan Times, March 18, 2005.
The Hindu, August 21, 2005.
The Hindu, September 18, 2005.
The Hindu, September 26, 2005.
The Hindu, October 6, 2005.
The Hindu, October 31, 2005.
The Hindu, January 26, 2006.

Websites

http://pd.cpim.org/
http://www.labour.nic.in
http://www.ilo.org./
www.google.com

Statutes

Beedi and Cigar Workers (Conditions of Employment) Act, 1966.
Building and Other Construction Workers' (Regulation of Employment and Conditions of Service) Act, 1996.
Child Labour (Prohibition and Regulation) Act, 1986.
Contract Labour (Regulation and Abolition) Act, 1970.
Dock Workers' (Regulation of Employment) Act, 1948.
Inter-State Migrant Workmen (Regulation of Employment and Conditions of Service) Act, 1979.
Minimum Wages Act, 1948.
Payment of Wages Act, 1936.
Plantation Labour Act, 1951.
The Factories Act, 1948.
The Bonded Labour System (Abolition) Act, 1976.
The Mines Act, 1952.
The National Rural Employment Guarantee Act, 2005.
Workmen's Compensation Act, 1923.

Index